MATH STARTERS

for Every Day of the School Year

by Karen D. Mancuso

SCHOLASTIC
PROFESSIONAL BOOKS

New York ✳ Toronto ✳ London ✳ Auckland ✳ Sydney

Mexico City ✳ New Delhi ✳ Hong Kong ✳ Buenos Aires

This book is dedicated to the memory of my grandmother
Dorothy May Byrnes
who has been my constant source
of laughter and love.

To my parents
Salvatore and Lois Mancuso
thank you for your continuous love and support.

Special thanks to Kathy Cermola, Susan Paradis, Geraldine Talge,
and all the students who pass
through my doorway.

Cover and interior design by Kelli Thompson
Cover and interior illustrations by Mike Moran

ISBN: 0-439-31753-3

Contents

	Page
Introduction	5
NCTM Standards Correlation Grid	6
Daily Problems	7–42

Number Sense
	Day
Place Value	1, 24, 47, 70, 93, 116, 139, 162
Pictorial Representations of Numbers	2, 25, 48, 71, 94, 117, 140, 163
Equivalent Fractions, Decimals, and Percents	3, 26, 49, 72, 95, 118, 141
Order, Magnitude, and Rounding of Numbers	4, 27, 50, 73, 96, 119, 142, 164

Operations
Models for Operations	5, 28, 51, 74, 97, 120, 143, 165
Computation With Whole Numbers and Decimals	6, 29, 52, 75, 98, 121, 144, 166
Computation With Fractions	7, 30, 53, 76, 99, 122, 145, 167
Word Problems	8, 31, 54, 77, 100, 123, 146, 168

Estimation and Approximation
Numerical Estimation Strategies	9, 32, 55, 78, 101, 124, 147, 169
Estimating Solutions to Problems	10, 33, 56, 79, 102, 125, 148, 170

Ratio, Proportion, and Percent
Ratios and Proportions	11, 34, 57, 80, 103, 126, 149
Computation With Percent	12, 35, 58, 81, 104, 127, 150

Measurement
Approximating Measures	13, 36, 59, 82, 105, 128, 151, 171
Customary and Metric Measures	14, 37, 60, 83, 106, 129, 152, 172
Perimeter, Area, and Volume	15, 38, 61, 84, 107, 130, 153, 173

Spatial Relationships
Geometric Shapes and Properties	16, 39, 62, 85, 108, 131, 154, 174
Spatial Relationships	17, 40, 63, 86, 109, 132, 155, 175

Probability and Statistics
Tables, Graphs, and Charts	18, 41, 64, 87, 110, 133, 156, 176
Statistics and Data Analysis	19, 42, 65, 88, 111, 134, 157, 177
Probability	20, 43, 66, 89, 112, 135, 158, 178

Patterns
Patterns	21, 44, 67, 90, 113, 136, 159

Algebra and Functions
Algebraic Concepts	22, 45, 68, 91, 114, 137, 160, 179

Discrete Mathematics
Classification and Logical Reasoning	23, 46, 69, 92, 115, 138, 161, 180

	Page
More Practice Worksheets	**43–71**

Number Sense
Place Value	43
Pictorial Representations of Numbers	44
Equivalent Fractions, Decimals, and Percents	45
Order, Magnitude, and Rounding of Numbers	46, 47

Operations
Models for Operations	48
Computation With Whole Numbers and Decimals	49
Computation With Fractions	50
Solving Word Problems	51, 52, 53

Estimation and Approximation
Numerical Estimation Strategies	54
Estimating Solutions to Problems	55

Ratio, Proportion, and Percent
Ratios and Proportions	56
Computation With Percent	57

Measurement
Approximating Measures	58
Customary and Metric Measures	59
Perimeter, Area, and Volume	60

Spatial Relationships
Geometric Shapes and Properties	61
Spatial Relationships	62, 63

Probability and Statistics
Tables, Graphs, and Charts	64
Statistics and Data Analysis	65, 66
Probability	67

Patterns
Patterns	68

Algebra and Functions
Algebraic Concepts	69, 70

Discrete Mathematics
Classification and Logical Reasoning	71

| **Answer Key** .... | **72–80** |

Introduction

How long does it take your class to settle down at the beginning of the period? Multiply that time by five days a week . . . twenty days a month . . . one hundred eighty days a year. That adds up to a lot of missed learning time, doesn't it?

Math Starters for Every Day of the School Year can help you regain that lost time. This book enables you to easily establish a daily routine of settling down to the business of math by providing you with an engaging problem for each day of the school year. I've organized the problems in a spiral format so that various mathematics skills and concepts are revisited seven to eight times throughout the school year. You can also choose problems to meet specific student needs by using the NCTM Standards Correlation Grid on page 6.

Solving the daily problems as a class is a great way to keep all students' math skills sharpened. Students can complete the starters independently, in pairs, or in small groups. However, you may want to reproduce the problem on a transparency for use with an overhead projector. Students can work from the screen or from individual copies you've given them. Encourage a discussion of the problem and its solution.

Each skill area has a companion Practice Worksheet that can be used for reinforcement. You may want to have students complete these worksheets independently, in pairs or in small groups. I also use them as assessment tools and for homework.

Because the skills featured are closely aligned with NCTM Principles and Standards for School Mathematics, Math Starters for Every Day of the School Year complements many math programs and textbooks.

Connection With the NCTM Standards 2000

	Number and Operations	Algebra	Geometry	Measurement	Data Analysis and Probability	Problem Solving	Reasoning and Proof	Communication	Connections	Representation
Place Value	X						X	X	X	X
Pictorial Representation	X						X	X	X	X
Equivalent Fractions, Decimals, and Percents	X						X	X	X	X
Order, Magnitude, and Rounding of Numbers	X					X	X	X	X	X
Models for Operations	X					X	X	X	X	X
Computation With Whole Numbers and Decimals	X	X					X	X	X	X
Computation With Fractions	X	X					X	X	X	X
Word Problems	X	X				X	X	X	X	X
Numerical Estimation Strategies	X						X	X	X	X
Estimating Solutions to Problems	X						X	X	X	X
Ratios and Proportions	X	X					X	X	X	X
Computation With Percent	X	X					X	X	X	X
Approximating Measures	X		X	X			X	X	X	X
Customary and Metric Measures	X			X			X	X	X	X
Perimeter, Area, and Volume	X	X	X	X			X	X	X	X
Geometric Shapes and Properties			X				X	X	X	X
Spatial Relationships			X				X	X	X	X
Tables, Graphs, and Charts	X			X	X		X	X	X	X
Statistics and Data Analysis	X	X		X	X		X	X	X	X
Probability	X			X	X		X	X	X	X
Patterns	X	X		X			X	X	X	X
Algebraic Concepts	X	X					X	X	X	X
Classification and Logical Reasoning	X					X	X	X	X	X

Name _____ Date _____

 Day 1

1. Write 3.15 + 4.7 + 0.6 in standard form. _____

2. Show 713.65 in expanded notation. _____

 Day 2

1. The shaded portion represents which fraction or mixed number?

Ⓐ $\frac{3}{4}$ Ⓑ $2\frac{1}{4}$ Ⓒ $2\frac{3}{4}$ Ⓓ $3\frac{1}{3}$

2. The shaded portion represents which decimal?

Ⓐ 0.103   Ⓑ 0.13   Ⓒ 1.03   Ⓓ 1.3

 Day 3

1. Which is equivalent to $2\frac{2}{8}$?

Ⓐ 2.25   Ⓑ 2.28   Ⓒ 2.3   Ⓓ 2.50

2. Which is equivalent to $\frac{3}{4}$?

Ⓐ 0.25   Ⓑ 0.34   Ⓒ 0.75   Ⓓ 3.4

 Day 4

Sales this year at Here's the Scoop Ice Cream Shop increased by $4832. Which statement **best** describes this increase?

Ⓐ   Sales increased about $4500.

Ⓑ   Sales increased about $4700.

Ⓒ   Sales increased about $4800.

Ⓓ   Sales increased about $5000.

 Day 5

Lauren purchased a CD player marked $159.99. The store had a sale, discounting all CD players 25%. Which number sentence would you use to determine how much she saved by buying the CD player on sale?

Ⓐ $159.99 + 0.25 =   Ⓒ $159.99 x 0.25 =

Ⓑ $159.99 − 0.25 =   Ⓓ $159.99 ÷ 0.25 =

Work Area

Day 6 Solve these problems.

1. 7068 + 1573 = _____   3. 736 × 9 = _____

2. 16,000 − 4388 = _____   4. 455 ÷ 7 = _____

Work Area

Day 7 Solve these problems.

1. $\frac{1}{2} + \frac{1}{2}$ = _____   3. $\frac{4}{6} - \frac{2}{6}$ = _____

2. $\frac{3}{8} + \frac{2}{4}$ = _____   4. $\frac{5}{9} - \frac{1}{3}$ = _____

Day 8

1. The stadium seats 8265 people. The stadium was sold out for the first four games of the season. **About** how many fans attended these games?

Ⓐ 8000   Ⓑ 16,000   Ⓒ 24,000   Ⓓ 32,000

2. Candy bars sell for $0.79 each. **About** how much will eight candy bars cost?

Ⓐ $4.80   Ⓑ $5.60   Ⓒ $6.40   Ⓓ $7.20

Day 9 Matthew wants to find the sum of 83 and 247. Show the numbers you would use to Estimate this amount. Solve and explain why you chose these numbers.

Estimate _____   _____

Solution _____

Explanation _____

Day 10 Christa wants to subtract 139 from 852. To get an estimate of this difference, which number sentence would be **best** for Christa to use?

Ⓐ 800 − 100 =   Ⓒ 900 − 100 =

Ⓑ 850 − 140 =   Ⓓ 140 − 850 =

Name _____ Date _____

Day 11 There are 15 boys and 9 girls in Mr. Hall's class. What is the ratio of boys to girls?

Ⓐ 5:3 Ⓑ 3:15 Ⓒ 24:1 Ⓓ 15:3

Day 12 Solve these problems.

1. 100% of 300 =

3. 1% of 300 =

2. 10% of 300 = _____

4. 11% of 300 = _____

Day 13 **1.** The measure of angle x appears to be **about** how many degrees?

Ⓐ 45° Ⓑ 65° Ⓒ 90° Ⓓ 115°

2. What type of angle is this? _____

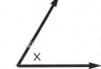

Day 14 **1.** What is the **best** unit to measure the length of a car?

Ⓐ inches Ⓒ miles
Ⓑ feet Ⓓ yards

2. The **best** unit to measure the length of a building is _____ .

Ⓐ millimeters Ⓒ meters
Ⓑ centimeters Ⓓ kilometers

Day 15 **About** how many small squares can fit in the larger figure? _____

Using the small square as a unit of 1, what is the perimeter of the larger figure? _____

Name _____ Date _____

 Day 16 Which of the following is **not** a quadrilateral?

Ⓐ   Ⓑ  Ⓒ   Ⓓ

Day 17 Draw the reflection of the letter E across the line.

Day 18 The table shows the number of students enrolled at four dance studios.

Dance Studio	Number of Students
All That Jazz	287
Tip of the Toe	312
Keep Moving	245
Stepping Out	364

On graph paper, draw and label a bar graph that represents the number of students at each dance studio.

Day 19 The table below shows the increase in video rentals from 2000 to 2002.

Video Store	2000	2002
Rent One	350,276	471,832
On the Reel	274,018	468,732
Movie Blast	110,627	341,254
Video Universe	98,703	248,576

Which video store had the largest increase in rentals from 2000 to 2002? _____

Day 20 If you tossed a coin 100 times, about how many times would it turn up tails? _____ Now toss a coin 100 times and see how many times it turns up tails. _____

Work Area

Day 21

1. What are the next three numbers in the sequence?

5, 7, 11, 17, _____, _____, _____

2. Draw the next two shapes.

 _____, _____

Day 22

Solve these problems.

1. $16 + 64 \div 8 =$ _____

2. $5n = 570 \quad n =$ _____

Day 23

The letters of the alphabet were written separately on a piece of paper and put into a bag. What is the likelihood that a vowel (a, e, i, o, u) would be pulled out of the bag on the first try? _____

Day 24

Fill in the table.

Number	0.1 more	0.1 less	0.01 more	0.01 less
23.48				
3.067				

Day 25

1. Shade 0.04 of this square.　**2.** Shade 0.7 of this square.

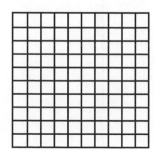　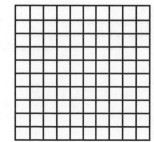

Day 26

1. Which is equivalent to 5.4?

Ⓐ $\frac{54}{100}$　　Ⓑ $\frac{20}{4}$　　Ⓒ $5\frac{2}{5}$　　Ⓓ $5\frac{5}{4}$

2. Write the fraction equivalent to each of the following decimals. Give your answer in simplest form.

0.25 = _____　　　　　　0.30 = _____

 Day 27

If you put 27.8 in the following lists and still kept the numbers in order from **smallest** to **largest**, in which list would 27.8 become the third number?

Ⓐ 27.3 28.5 28.9　　　　Ⓒ 27.75 27.85 27.95

Ⓑ 27.06 27.07 27.09　　Ⓓ 27.46 27.78 27.92

 Day 28

1. There are 96 students going on a field trip to the zoo. If there are 12 chaperones, which number sentence would you use to determine how many students would be in each group?

Ⓐ 96 + 12 =　　　　　Ⓒ 96 × 12 =

Ⓑ 96 − 12 =　　　　　Ⓓ 96 ÷ 12 =

2. How many students will be in each group? _____

 Day 29

Solve these problems.

1. $78.07 + $37.96 = _____　　**3.** $4.16 × 18 = _____

2. $47.39 − $9.78 = _____　　**4.** 14.406 ÷ 6 = _____

 Day 30

Solve these problems.

1. $\frac{3}{16} + \frac{7}{8}$ = _____　　**3.** $1 - \frac{3}{4}$ = _____

2. $8 \times \frac{3}{4}$ = _____　　**4.** $\frac{9}{10} + \frac{4}{10}$ = _____

Work Area

Name _____ Date _____

 Day 31 Kathy placed her puppies on a scale to see how much each one weighed. Their weights were $3\frac{3}{4}$ lbs, $4\frac{2}{3}$ lbs, and $4\frac{1}{3}$ lbs. **About** how much was the total weight of the 3 puppies?

ⓐ 8 lbs   ⓑ 11 lbs   ⓒ 13 lbs   ⓓ 17 lbs

Work Area

Day 32 **1.** Tasha wants to find the product of 59 and 906. Show the numbers you would use to **estimate** this product. Then solve.

Estimate _____   _____

Solution _____

2. Brad wants to add $\frac{4}{7} + \frac{8}{9}$. To get a good **estimate** of this sum, which example would be **best** for Brad to use?

ⓐ $\frac{1}{2} + \frac{1}{2} =$ ⓒ $\frac{1}{2} + 1 =$

ⓑ $0 + 1 =$ ⓓ $1 + 1 =$

 Day 33 Susie wants to find 52% of 273. Show the numbers you would use to **estimate** this value. Solve and explain why you used these numbers.

Estimate _____   _____

Solution _____

Explanation _____

Day 34 There are 18 boys and 12 girls in Mrs. Joy's homeroom. What is the ratio of girls to boys?

ⓐ 2:3   ⓑ 18:6   ⓒ 6:18   ⓓ 3:2

  Day 35 Solve these problems.

1. 100% of 251 = _____   **3.** 1% of 251 = _____

2. 10% of 251 = _____   **4.** 121% of 251 = _____

Name _____   Date _____

 Day 36 Approximately how long is an unsharpened #2 pencil?

Ⓐ 10 mm   Ⓑ 3 cm   Ⓒ 7 cm   Ⓓ 19 cm

 Day 37 Complete each statement.

1. 1 gallon = _____ half gallons

2. 1 gallon = _____ quarts

3. 1 quart = _____ pints

4. 1 pint = _____ cups

 Day 38 Use your ruler to determine the area, in square centimeters, of the figure shown. _____

 Day 39 **1.** Which is not a rectangle?

  Ⓐ   Ⓑ   Ⓒ   Ⓓ

2. How many degrees does a rectangle have? _____

 Day 40 **1.** Which letter has a line of symmetry?

Ⓐ S   Ⓑ E   Ⓒ R   Ⓓ J

2. Write as many words as you can that contain all symmetrical letters. (The word must be written with capital letters.)

_____

_____

_____

Name _____ Date _____

Day 41 The table shows the number of golfers that have memberships at four country clubs.

Country Club	Number of Members
First Swing Country Club	1,742
On the Green Country Club	1,618
Stonebrook Country Club	1,788
Grassy Knoll Country Club	1,529

On graph paper, draw and label a bar graph that represents the number of members at each country club.

Day 42 The 2002 salaries for some local officials are listed below.

Official	Salary	Official	Salary
Hines	$66,500	Martino	$48,960
Cleary	$83,427	Gibson	$64,918

1. Which two officials have a combined salary **closest** to $150,000? _____
2. Whose salary is **closest** to $65,000? _____

Day 43 You have 3 quarters, 3 dimes, and 4 nickels in your pocket. If you pull out one coin without looking, what is the probability that it will be a nickel? Show your answer as a ratio, fraction, and percent.

_____   _____   _____

Day 44 What are the next three numbers in the sequence?

56 , 48 , 40 , 32 , _____ , _____ , _____

Day 45 Solve these problems.

1. $7^2 + 3 \times 6 =$ _____   **2.** $(5 + 11)\frac{3}{4} =$ _____

Name _____ Date _____

Day 46 There are 4 numbered tiles in a bag. If you took 3 tiles out and added them together, which sum would you **not** make?

Ⓐ 15   Ⓑ 17   Ⓒ 18   Ⓓ 19

Day 47 Solve these problems.

1. 8.56 x 100 = _____   **2.** 6.3 x 10,000 = _____

Day 48 The hexagon contains solid and striped shapes.

1. What percent of the shapes are striped?
Ⓐ 20% Ⓑ 30%   Ⓒ 40%   Ⓓ 60%

2. What percent of the shapes are solid?
Ⓐ 20% Ⓑ 30%   Ⓒ 40%   Ⓓ 60%

Day 49 Which is equivalent to 0.64?

Ⓐ $\frac{1}{3}$ Ⓑ $\frac{30}{50}$ Ⓒ $\frac{16}{25}$ Ⓓ $\frac{6}{8}$

Day 50 **1.** Which letter **best** shows $\frac{7}{8}$ on the number line? _____

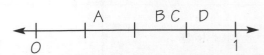

2. The class scored between 75% and 90% on their math test. On the number line, shade in the appropriate range for the test scores.

Name _____ Date _____

 Day 51

1. Mr. Hood wants to buy ice cream bars for his five reading classes. He has a total of 112 students. If each box contains 24 ice cream bars, which number sentence would you use to determine how many boxes Mr. Hood should buy?

Ⓐ   112 + 24 =   Ⓒ   112 x 24 =

Ⓑ   112 − 24 =   Ⓓ   112 ÷ 24 =

2. How many boxes must Mr. Hood buy so that each of his students would get an ice cream bar? _____

 Day 52

Solve these problems.

1. 6.8 + 17.35 + 0.475 = _____   **3.** 2.73 x 0.45 = _____

2. 175.4 − 63.37 = _____   **4.** $18.27 ÷ 3 = _____

 Day 53

Solve these problems.

1. $2\frac{1}{2} + 9\frac{1}{4} =$ _____   **3.** $8 - 2\frac{3}{5} =$ _____

2. $5\frac{3}{9} + \frac{1}{3} =$ _____   **4.** $7\frac{2}{3} - 4 =$ _____

 Day 54

The coach ordered 4 large pizzas for her basketball players. There are 16 slices per pizza. At the end of the party, this is what was left:

$\frac{1}{4}$ of the sausage pizza $\frac{1}{8}$ of the pepperoni pizza

$\frac{2}{4}$ of the onion & pepper pizza $\frac{1}{16}$ of the cheese pizza

What was the total number of pizza slices that were left?_____

 Day 55

Madison wants to subtract $\frac{4}{10}$ from $\frac{4}{5}$. To get a good **estimate** of this difference, which example would be **best** for Madison to use?

Ⓐ   4 − 4   Ⓑ $1 - \frac{1}{2}$ Ⓒ $\frac{1}{2} - 1$ Ⓓ   1 − 1

Day 56 Dominque wants to find the sum of 8.05 and 16.6. Show the whole numbers you would use to **estimate** this amount. Find the estimated sum and explain why you chose these numbers.

Work Area

Estimate _____   _____

Solution _____

Explanation _____

Day 57 1. In Joshua's dresser, the ratio of shirts to jeans is 5:3. He has 15 shirts. How many pair of jeans does he have?

Ⓐ 3   Ⓑ 9   Ⓒ 27   Ⓓ 45

2. In Stephanie's sock drawer, the ratio of white socks to design socks is 3:4. She has 16 pairs of design socks. How many pairs of white socks does she have? _____

Day 58 Solve these problems.

1. 10% of 48 = _____   **3.** 20% of 48 = _____

2. 50% of 48 = _____   **4.** 23% of 48 = _____

Day 59 How many degrees are there in each angle?

1. right angle = _____   **5.** obtuse angle = _____

2. straight angle = _____   **6.** circle = _____

3. triangle = _____   **7.** square = _____

4. acute angle = _____   **8.** rectangle = _____

Day 60 Change each metric unit. Use the abbreviation chart as a guide: **km hm dkm m dm cm mm**

1. 2 km = _____ m   **4.** 72 m = _____ dkm

2. 90 cm = _____ m   **5.** 2.6 mm = _____ cm

3. 180 m = _____ mm

Name _____ Date _____

Day 61 Draw at least 3 polygons that have an area of 8 square units?

Day 62

1. Which figure is **not** a pentagon?

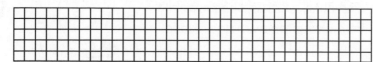

Ⓐ   Ⓑ   Ⓒ   Ⓓ

2. hexagon = _____ sides   3. octagon = _____ sides

Day 63 How many different parallelograms can you draw?
Show all lines of symmetry with each figure.

Day 64 The table shows the number of members in four book clubs.

Book Club	Members	Book Club	Members
The Binding	810	Flip the Page	761
Cover to Cover	527	Bookmark	693

On graph paper, draw and label a bar graph that represents the number of members of each book club.

Day 65 The graph shows the results of a survey conducted in Ms. Greene's and Mr. Brown's classes.

What Is Your Favorite Subject?

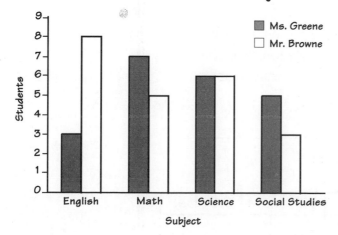

Which subject shows the biggest difference between classes? _____   What is the difference? _____

Name _____ Date _____

Day 66 Four cards, one of each suit, are placed facedown on a table. If you turned over only one card, what is the probability of that card being hearts? Show your answer as a ratio, fraction, and percent.

_____   _____   _____

Day 67 What are the next two numbers or shapes in these sequences?

1. 4, 9, 16, 25, 36, _____ , _____

What is the tenth number? _____

Describe the pattern _____

2.   , _____ , _____

Explain how you decided what to draw _____

Day 68 Solve these problems.

1. $x + \dfrac{2}{7} = \dfrac{5}{14}$

Ⓐ $\dfrac{1}{14}$ Ⓑ $\dfrac{4}{14}$ Ⓒ $\dfrac{5}{14}$ Ⓓ $\dfrac{3}{7}$

2. $\dfrac{2}{5} + x = \dfrac{10}{15}$

Ⓐ $\dfrac{4}{15}$ Ⓑ $\dfrac{6}{15}$ Ⓒ $\dfrac{5}{10}$ Ⓓ $\dfrac{8}{10}$

Day 69 Number tiles 1–10 were put into a bag. What is the likelihood that an even tile would be pulled out of the bag on the first try? Show your answer as a ratio, fraction, and percent.

_____   _____   _____

Day 70 Fill in the table.

Number	0.1 more	0.1 less	0.01 more	0.01 less
85.14				
42.09				

Name _____ Date _____

1. Shade 1.24   **2.** Shade 0.17

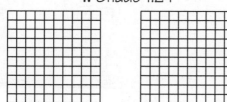   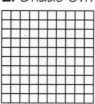

Work Area

3. Show each decimal as a percent. _____ _____

1. Three sixths of Mr. Edward's class brought their lunches to school. What percentage of the class was that?

Ⓐ 9%   Ⓑ 36%   Ⓒ 50%   Ⓓ 80%

2. If Mr. Edward has 36 students in his class, how many brought their lunch to school? _____

The table below lists the four top students in the hula hoop contest and their times.

Name	Time	Name	Time
Alyssa	15 min. 28 sec.	Carmine	15 min. 58 sec.
Rachel	16 min. 12 sec.	Luisa	16 min. 34 sec.

What is the **best** way to describe Alyssa's time for the hula hoop contest?

Ⓐ a little less than $15\frac{1}{2}$ minutes

Ⓑ a little less than 16 minutes

Ⓒ a little more than 15 minutes

Ⓓ a little more than 16 minutes

Austin can save 30% on expenses for his trip to Orlando. The trip costs $1250. Write a number sentence to figure out how much he will save on his trip. Then solve.

_____

Solve these problems.

1. 762.1 + 45 + 91.27 = _____   **3.** 40.7 × 8.2 = _____

2. 4 − 2.324 = _____   **4.** 3755 ÷ 0.5 = _____

Name _____ Date _____

Day 76 Solve these problems.

1. $11\frac{1}{12} + 4\frac{3}{4} =$ _____   3. $43\frac{3}{5} - 25\frac{4}{5} =$ _____

2. $10 - 1\frac{6}{10} =$ _____   4. $\frac{1}{3} \times \frac{3}{10} =$ _____

Day 77 Based on the drawing, approximately how long is the stem of the flower? _____

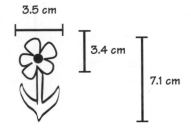

3.5 cm

3.4 cm

7.1 cm

Day 78 1. Donna needs to divide 4906 by 111. To get a good estimate of this quotient, which number sentence would be **best** for Donna to use? Then solve the problem.

Ⓐ 4900 ÷ 10 = _____   Ⓒ 5000 ÷ 10 = _____

Ⓑ 4900 ÷ 100 = _____   Ⓓ 4000 ÷ 100 = _____

2. Andre needs to find the product of $9\frac{1}{3}$ and $8\frac{3}{4}$. Show the numbers you would use to estimate this product, then solve.

Estimate _____   _____

Solution _____

Day 79 Ivy wants to find 31% of 949. Show the numbers she should use to estimate this value, then solve.

Estimate _____   _____

Solution _____

Day 80 The ratio of dogs to cats at the Kalroy Kennel is 7:2. There are 14 cats. How many dogs are there? _____

Work Area

Day 81 There are 2 circles, 2 hexagons, 4 squares, and 8 triangles drawn on the board. What percent of the shapes are:

1. circles _____   **3.** squares _____

2. hexagons _____   **4.** triangles _____

Day 82 A rectangular prism has been filled with sand. What is the **approximate** volume of the prism if the measurements are 30.4 cm × 9.7 cm × 8.2 cm? _____

Day 83 Philip used 3.5 gallons of paint to paint both the hallway and the playroom.

How many quarts did he use? _____

How many pints did he use? _____

Day 84 **1.** Use your ruler to determine the **approximate** perimeter and area, in centimeters, of this scalene right triangle.

Perimeter – _____

Area = _____

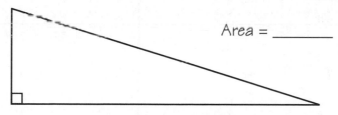

2. How many degrees does a triangle have? _____

3. In the following triangles, how many sides are the same length?

scalene = _____ sides the same length

isosceles = _____ sides the same length

equilateral = _____ sides the same length

Day 85 Draw the following polygons:
quadrilateral, octagon, pentagon, parallelogram,
equilateral triangle, isosceles triangle, scalene triangle

Day 86 Which is shown with a line of symmetry?

Ⓐ

Ⓒ

Ⓑ

Ⓓ

Work Area

Day 87 Use the data below to construct a line graph showing the possible number of swimmers who used the Pebble Public Pool over a four-year period.

• Swimmers increased by $\frac{1}{2}$ between year 1 and year 4.

• Swimmers dropped slightly in year 3.

• Yearly number of swimmers was never less than 1600.

Day 88 The table shows at what speeds 4 drivers were traveling.

Driver	Speed
Alicia	65.0 mph
Kaitlyn	60.8 mph
Connor	62.5 mph
Collin	59.7 mph

What was the average speed of the drivers? _____

Day 89 There are 5 red marbles, 3 orange marbles, and 2 blue marbles in a bag. If you choose one marble without looking, what is the probability that it will be red?

Ⓐ 5%   Ⓑ 10%   Ⓒ 15%   Ⓓ 50%

Day 90 Draw the next shape in the sequence.

 _____

Explain how you decided what to draw. _____

_____

Name _____ Date _____

Day 91 Solve these problems.

1. $(7 + 5) \div \frac{6}{10}$ = _____   **3.** $17.40 = 1.5n$ _____

2. $5^2 \div \frac{5}{7}$ = _____   **4.** $\frac{n}{23} = 8$ _____

Work Area

Day 92 Ms. Beja's class received their midterm grades. Use the following information to answer the questions below.

• The number of C's earned was three times the number of A's.

• The number of B's earned was equal to the sum of the number of A's and C's.

• There were 6 D's and no F's.

• The number of B's earned was twice the number of D's.

1. How many students received . . .

A's? _____   B's? _____   C's? _____   D's? _____

2. How many students are in Ms. Beja's class? _____

Day 93 **1.** Write $0.32 + 0.5 + 2$ in standard form. _____

2. Show 5.63 in expanded notation. _____

Day 94 **1.** How much of this shape is shaded? **2.** Shade $\frac{3}{5}$ of the shape.

fraction _____ decimal _____

Day 95 **1.** Which is equivalent to $10\frac{5}{50}$?

Ⓐ $\frac{10}{2}$ Ⓑ $5\frac{7}{10}$ Ⓒ $\frac{50}{5}$ Ⓓ 10.1

2. Twenty-eight percent of the houses on Lake Drive are yellow. What fraction of the houses is that?

Ⓐ $\frac{7}{25}$ Ⓑ $\frac{14}{100}$ Ⓒ $\frac{7}{50}$ Ⓓ $\frac{28}{10}$

Name _____ Date _____

 Day 96 Diego came to school with $\frac{4}{5}$ of his math work complete, $\frac{2}{3}$ of his science work complete, and $\frac{2}{5}$ of his social studies work complete.

Rank the fractions from smallest to largest.

_____   _____   _____

Work Area

Day 97 **1.** Cliff wants to buy an alarm clock that costs $39.99. He has a coupon to receive $10.00 off any purchase. Which number sentence should Cliff use to determine the cost of the alarm clock?

Ⓐ $39.99 + $10.00 =   Ⓒ $39.99 x $10.00 =
Ⓑ $39.99 - $10.00 =   Ⓓ $39.99 ÷ $10.00 =

2. There is 6% sales tax. What will the alarm clock cost after the discount and with tax? _____

Day 98 Use mental math to solve these problems.

1. 740 x 100 = _____   **4.** 740 ÷ 10 = _____

2. 1000 x 63 = _____   **5.** 630 ÷ 100 = _____

3. 10 x 5.8 = _____   **6.** 5.8 ÷ 1,000 = _____

 Day 99 Solve these problems.

1. $2\frac{4}{7}$ x 21 = _____   **2.** $3 \times 1\frac{5}{9}$ = _____

 Day 100 **1.** Monica purchased 2 CDs for $17.99 each and a book for $8.95. She gave the sales clerk a fifty-dollar bill. If there is no tax, did Monica have enough money for this purchase? Show or explain how you got your answer.

_____

2. Steve earns approximately $88 every month on his paper route. If he continues to make the same amount each month, **about** how much will he earn in a year? Show or explain how you got your answer.

_____

1. Michelle wanted to **estimate** the product of 59 and 896, so she multiplied 60 x 900. Was Michelle's estimate more or less than the actual product? Explain your reasoning.

Work Area

_____

_____

2. Robert wanted to **estimate** the difference of 2.098 and 7.32, so he subtracted 2 from 7. Was Robert's estimate more or less than the actual difference? Explain your reasoning.

_____

_____

 Mr. Pickett purchased 600 feet of fencing to enclose the pool area in his backyard. The space he wants to enclose is 215 ft long by 110 ft wide. Explain how you could use estimation to decide if he bought enough fencing.

_____

_____

 1. In Mrs. Glick's class there are 9 tables and 27 chairs. What is the ratio of tables to chairs?

Ⓐ 4.5:9 Ⓑ 2:7 Ⓒ 3:18 Ⓓ 1:3

2. In Mr. Rivera's homeroom there are 16 boys and 12 girls. What is the ratio of girls to boys?

Ⓐ 3:4 Ⓑ 2:8 Ⓒ 3:7 Ⓓ 5:9

$$\frac{part}{whole} = \frac{\%}{100}$$

1. What is 35% of 84? _____   **2.** What is 9% of 48? _____

 Estimate the measure of each angle.

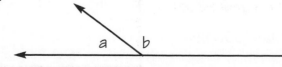

a= _____

b= _____

Name _____ Date _____

Work Area

Day 106

1. Of the units listed, which is the smallest unit for measuring weight?

Ⓐ ton   Ⓑ ounce   Ⓒ pound

2. Which unit would you use to measure the weight of your math book? _____

Day 107

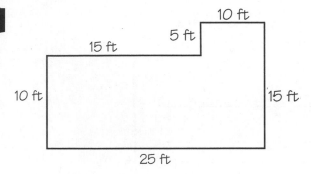

10 ft

5 ft

15 ft

10 ft

15 ft

25 ft

1. What is the area of this figure?_____

2. What is the perimeter of this figure?_____

Day 108

What does "congruent" mean? _____
In the work area, draw the shape that is congruent to each of the shapes below.

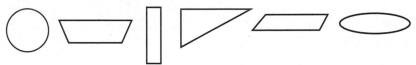

Day 109

What does "similar" mean? _____
In the work area, draw the shape that is similar to each of the shapes above.

Day 110

Use the data below to construct a line graph showing the amount of coffee consumed at Perk-a-Bean Coffee Shop over a four year period.

• Consumption of coffee increased by $\frac{1}{3}$ between year 2 and year 4.

• Consumption of coffee increased slightly in year 3.

• Consumption of coffee was never less than 1500 cups per year.

Name _____ Date _____

 Day 111 The table shows how long each student studied for a social studies test.

Student	Minutes
Ryan	43
Tim	37
Elizabeth	25
Calvin	40
Lois	35

1. What is the mean time for studying? _____

2. What is the median time? _____

 Day 112 The spinner was spun. It landed on blue. If it is spun again, what is the probability that the arrow will land on blue?

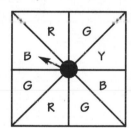

Ⓐ $\frac{1}{4}$ Ⓑ $\frac{1}{2}$ Ⓒ $\frac{1}{3}$ Ⓓ $\frac{3}{4}$

Day 113 What are the next four numbers in the sequence?

18, 36, 54, _____, _____, _____, _____

Day 114 Write in mathematical form . . .

1. the sum of a number and 9.
Ⓐ $n + 9$ Ⓑ $9 - n$ Ⓒ $9n$ Ⓓ $n - 9$

2. 18 less than 4 times Ted's height.
Ⓐ $4t + 18$ Ⓑ $18t - 4$ Ⓒ $4t - 18$ Ⓓ $18 - 40t$

Day 115 Place the following letters into two groups. Describe what each group has in common.

A   B   C   D   E   F   G   H

Name _____ Date _____

Day 116

1. Write 0.92 + 4 + 3.8 in standard form. _____

2. Show 106.007 in expanded notation. _____

Day 117

1. Shade $\frac{4}{10}$ of the shape.

2. What percent of this shape is shaded? _____

Day 118

1. Belinda walked 20% farther on Tuesday than on Sunday. She walked 5 miles on Sunday. How far did she walk on Tuesday?

Ⓐ 5.5 mi   Ⓑ 6 mi   Ⓒ 7 mi   Ⓓ 7.5 mi

2. John purchased a new bike helmet. How much tax did he pay on a $20 helmet if the tax rate is 4%?

Ⓐ $0.20   Ⓑ $0.40   Ⓒ $0.50   Ⓓ $0.80

What was the total cost of his purchase? _____

Day 119

1. Which decimal, rounded to the nearest whole number, gives you 9?

Ⓐ 8.459   Ⓑ 9.459   Ⓒ 9.549   Ⓓ 8.294

2. Write these decimals on the lines below from greatest to least.

27.063   27.154   27.08   27.0976   27.17

_____   _____   _____   _____   _____

Day 120

1. MaryBeth was trying to figure out 20% of $350. Write a number sentence that will help MaryBeth solve this problem, then solve. _____

2. It costs Mr. Cermola $22 a month to have his garbage picked up. How much does it cost him a year? Write a number sentence to solve this problem, then solve.

_____

Name _____ Date _____

 Day 121

1. Ten packages of crayons cost $39.00. How much does one package cost?

  Ⓐ $0.39   Ⓑ $3.90   Ⓒ $39.00   Ⓓ $390.00

2. How much would one hundred packages of crayons cost?

  Ⓐ $390.00 Ⓑ $39.00   Ⓒ $3.90   Ⓓ $0.39

 Day 122

Solve these problems.

$$3\frac{2}{8} + 4\frac{9}{16} + \frac{1}{2} = \underline{\hspace{1cm}} \qquad (4\frac{5}{6} - 1\frac{5}{12}) - 2\frac{3}{9} = \underline{\hspace{1cm}}$$

 Day 123

Write a story problem for each of the following equations.

3.50 x 5 = M $25.44 ÷ 6 = M

 Day 124

1. Juan needs to divide 17 by $4\frac{7}{8}$. Show the numbers you would use to estimate this quotient. Solve, and explain why you chose these numbers.

Estimate _____   _____

Solution _____

Explanation _____

2. Paul wanted to **estimate** 78% of 37, so he calculated 80% of 40. Was Paul's estimate more or less than the actual answer? Explain your reasoning.

_____

_____

 Day 125

Mrs. Applebee bought fabric to make a tablecloth for her picnic table. Her table is 4 feet by 10 feet. The fabric measures 1.5 yards by 3 yards. Did she buy enough fabric? Explain.

_____

_____

Work Area

Day 126

1. There are 10 chocolate chip cookies and 15 peanut butter cookies in the cookie jar. What is the ratio of chocolate chip cookies to peanut butter cookies? _____

2. You have 3 quarters and 1 nickel in your pocket. What is the probability of pulling out a quarter from your pocket on the first try? Give the answer in the form of a percent.
_____

Day 127

Solve these problems.

1. What is 35% of 30? _____

2. What is 9% of 75? _____

3. 18 is what percent of 75? _____

Day 128

A cylinder has a radius of 2.5 cm and a height of 13 cm. What is the **approximate** volume of the cylinder? _____

Day 129

You're purchasing fencing for your backyard. The length of each piece of fence is 6 feet. To enclose your yard you'll need 45 pieces of fencing. How many yards of fencing will you need to purchase?

Ⓐ 45 yds   Ⓑ 90 yds   Ⓒ 120 yds   Ⓓ 360 yds

Day 130

How many square feet is the area of the figure below? _____

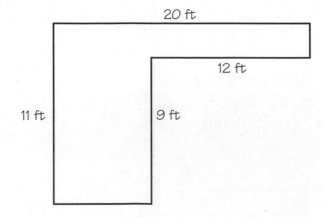

20 ft

12 ft

11 ft

9 ft

Name _____ Date _____

Day 131 Draw a circle that is inside a square, which is inside a trapezoid. Make sure your figure can have a line of symmetry and show it.

Day 132

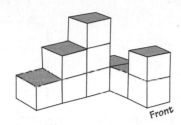

Front

Which example below **best** represents the front of this 3-dimensional shape?

Ⓐ   Ⓑ   Ⓒ   Ⓓ

Day 133 Use a stem-and-leaf plot to order the following numbers of hours students watched TV during a 10-day school vacation:
32, 57, 31, 24, 53, 26, 37, 41, 39, 51, 47, 29, 33

Day 134 The table shows the prices of four different DVD players.

DVD	Price
Brand A	$299
Brand B	$370
Brand C	$219
Brand D	$358

What is the mean price? _____

Day 135 Which would be a **reasonable** statement about the spinner?

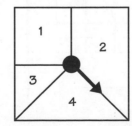

Ⓐ   The arrow has the same chance of landing on 2 and 3.

Ⓑ   The arrow will land on 1 more times than on 2.

Ⓒ   The arrow has an equal chance of landing on 1 and 4.

Ⓓ   The arrow will land on 3 twice as many times as on 1.

Day 136 If the pattern is continued, what will be the next three numbers?

4, 4, 8, 12, 20, 32, _____, _____, _____

What will be the eleventh term in this sequence? _____

Work Area

Day 137 Write in mathematical form.

1. 5 times a number increased by 2

Ⓐ 5n + 2   Ⓑ 5 x 2   Ⓒ 5 + 2n   Ⓓ 5n + 5

2. $\frac{3}{4}$ of the quantity 16 more than 3n

Ⓐ $3(\frac{3}{4}n + 16)$ Ⓒ $\frac{3}{4}(3n - 16)$

Ⓑ $\frac{3}{4}(3n + 16)$ Ⓓ $\frac{3}{4}n + 16$

Day 138 Place the numbers into two groups. Describe what each group has in common.

1   2   3   4   5   6   7   8   9   10

Day 139 Solve these problems.

1. 5.196×10^5 = _____   **3.** $365.2 \div 10^2$ = _____

2. 49.5×10^1 = _____   **4.** $584 \div 10^4$ = _____

Day 140 **1.** Shade 0.2 of the shape.   **2.** Shade 75% of the shape.

   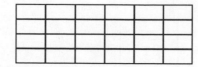

3. What percent of this shape is **not** shaded? _____

Name _____ Date _____

 1. Karelyn went to the store to buy a bag of potato chips. The chips cost $3.99. She had a coupon to save 25% on her purchase. **Approximately** how much did she spend?

Ⓐ $1.00   Ⓑ $3.00   Ⓒ $3.25   Ⓓ $4.25

2. What fraction represents Karelyn's savings?

Ⓐ $\frac{1}{25}$ Ⓑ $\frac{1}{4}$ Ⓒ $\frac{3}{5}$ Ⓓ $\frac{6}{7}$

Work Area

 The table shows the time earned, in seconds, by the four top runners for the 100-meter dash at the Women's Hexagon Open.

Runner	Time	Runner	Time
Terri	11.52	Lindsey	12.37
Alyson	11.5	Chelsea	11.08

1. Which of the times would round to 12 if you rounded to the whole number?_____

2. Rank the times from quickest to slowest.

_____   _____   _____   _____

 Joe needs to find the product of $6\frac{1}{4}$ and $4\frac{4}{5}$. Show a number sentence you would use to solve this problem. Solve this problem two different ways.

_____

_____

 Solve these problems.

1. $37.9 \times 10^4 =$ _____

3. $379 \div 10^2 =$ _____

2. $10^3 \times 0.19 =$ _____

4. $19 \div 10^1 =$ _____

 Solve these problems.

1. $2\frac{1}{3} \times 3\frac{2}{3} =$ _____

2. $5\frac{3}{5} \times 6\frac{1}{4}$ _____

Name _____ Date _____

 Day 146 Write a story problem for each of the following equations.

$$\frac{1}{2} \times \frac{3}{4} = M \qquad\qquad 36.28 \div 0.5 = M$$

Work Area

Day 147 1. Eleanor wants to **estimate** the cost per liter of a 3-liter bottle of soda that costs $1.89. What would be a good **estimate?** _____ Explain how you arrived at this answer.

_____

_____

2. Taryn wants to **estimate** the cost per pound of a 2-pound can of coffee that costs $12.49. What would be a good **estimate?** _____ Explain how you arrived at this answer.

_____

_____

Day 148 Mr. Mason purchased 64 square meters of brick for his patio. The width of the patio is 7.6 m and the length is 9.5 m. Explain how you could use estimation to decide if he bought enough brick.

_____

Day 149 Solve for n.

1. $\frac{15}{25} = \frac{n}{75}$ _____   3. $\frac{n}{7} = \frac{28}{49}$ _____

2. $\frac{5}{n} = \frac{8}{56}$ _____   4. $\frac{8}{96} = \frac{12}{n}$ _____

Day 150 Solve these problems.

1. What is 40% of 80? _____

2. What percent of 850 is 238? _____

3. 51 is what percent of 340? _____

Name _____ Date _____

  What is the **approximate** volume and surface area of a rectangular prism that has the following dimensions:
3.6" by 3.6" by 23.2"

Volume = _____   Surface Area = _____

  You can find out how old a tree is by counting the rings, beginning in the center and working your way out to the bark. This distance is called the

 Ⓐ chord   Ⓒ circumference

 Ⓑ diameter   Ⓓ radius

  Give the volume of each 3-dimensional shape.

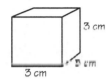

3 cm

3 cm   3 cm   5.5 cm

26.5 cm   12 cm

Volume = _____   Volume = _____

  Draw a polygon with a perimeter of 8 units and an area of 3 square units.

Draw a polygon with a perimeter of 18 units and an area of 9 square units.

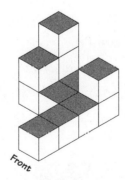

Front

Which example below **best** represents the front of this 3-dimensional shape?

Ⓐ   Ⓑ   Ⓒ   Ⓓ

Work Area

Name _____ Date _____

 Day 156 Use a stem-and-leaf plot to order a student's math grades for the first marking period:
82, 78, 89, 63, 98, 85, 95, 88, 76, 95, 79, 87, 88

 Day 157 Mrs. Bell kept track of how many telephone calls she received each day during one work week.

Day	Number of Calls
Monday	4
Tuesday	3
Wednesday	4
Thursday	8
Friday	7

1. What is the mean number of phone calls? _____

2. What is the median number of phone calls? _____

 Day 158 Which would be a **reasonable** statement about the marbles in the bag?

You are . . .
Ⓐ more likely to pull out a black marble than a gray one.
Ⓑ less likely to pull out a white marble than a gray one.
Ⓒ more likely to pull out a gray marble than a white one.
Ⓓ more likely to pull out a gray marble than a black one.

Day 159 What are the next four letters in the sequence?
A, Z, D, W, G, _____, _____, _____, _____

Day 160 An electrician charges $55 for the first hour and R for each additional hour. Which expression shows the correct charge for an 8-hour job?
Ⓐ 55 − 7R   Ⓑ 55R + 8   Ⓒ 8R + 55   Ⓓ 55 + 7R

Work Area

Name _____ Date _____

Work Area

Day 161 Place the following animals into two groups. Describe what each group has in common.

tiger	eagle	monkey
elephant	bear	giraffe
ostrich	horse	alligator

Day 162 Solve these problems.

1. $10^2 \times 6.089 =$ _____   **3.** $98.41 \div 10^4 =$ _____

2. $10^3 \times 32.774 =$ _____   **4.** $8214.62 \div 10^3 =$ _____

Day 163 **1.** Shade 40% of the shape.   **2.** Shade 25% of the shape.

3. What fraction of the circles is **not** shaded? _____

Day 164 **1.** Jamal jogged $4\frac{5}{8}$ miles on Monday, $4\frac{2}{3}$ miles on Wednesday, and $4\frac{3}{4}$ miles on Friday. List the distances from least to greatest. _____   _____   _____

2. What is the actual distance that Jamal jogged? _____

Day 165 **1.** Catherine purchased a pair of sneakers priced at $70. She received 10% off the price of the sneakers because she had a coupon. Write a number sentence to find her savings.

_____

2. Tax on Catherine's purchase is 6%. Write a number sentence to find the tax. With tax, what is the total price that she paid for the sneakers?

_____

Name _____ Date _____

 1. Whitney purchased 5 CDs for $60. The store took 10% off any purchase over $50. How much did Whitney save on the 5 CDs?

  Ⓐ $0.06   Ⓑ $0.60   Ⓒ $6.00   Ⓓ $600.00

2. With the discount, what is the price of the CDs?

  Ⓐ $54.00   Ⓑ $58.60   Ⓒ $64.00   Ⓓ $66.00

 Solve this problem.

$$\frac{12}{15} \times \frac{10}{9} \times \frac{4}{8} \times \frac{6}{10} \times \frac{25}{40} = \underline{\hspace{2cm}}$$

 1. Chris left for work at 7:25 A.M. It took him 35 minutes to get to work. He worked for 3 hours and 45 minutes. Then he took 45 minutes off for lunch. After lunch he worked 3 hours and 30 minutes. It took him 35 minutes to get home. What time was it when he had lunch? _____

What time was it when he got home? _____

2. Holly and her sister Sharon have to take turns doing the household chores. Holly says, "I know what we can do. Every day that the date is an even number, I'll do the chores and every day that the date is an odd number, you can do them." Is this a fair plan? _____

Show or explain how you got your answers. _____

_____

 Cassandra wants to **estimate** the cost per ounce of a 13.25 ounce bag of potato chips that cost $3.19. What would be a good **estimate**? _____
Explain how you arrived at your answer. _____

_____

 Virginia purchased 8 pounds of jelly beans. They cost $1.29 per pound. About how much did the jelly beans cost?

  Ⓐ $7.50   Ⓑ $10.40   Ⓒ $12.90   Ⓓ $16.00

Name _____ Date _____

Day 171

1. If a side of the square is 4 centimeters, then the length of the rectangle is _____ cm.

2. How many times larger is the rectangle than the square? _____

Day 172 Pearl purchased 270 liters of soda.

1. How many 3-liter bottles would that be? _____

2. How many 2-liter bottles would that be? _____

3. How many 1-liter bottles would that be? _____

Day 173 Find the volume of each cylinder.

1. diameter = 14 cm
height = 20 cm
Volume = _____

2. diameter = 3 m
height = 7 m
Volume = _____

Day 174 Draw all the possible rectangles that have an area of 36 square units. Show the dimensions next to each rectangle. Which rectangle has the largest perimeter? _____ Which rectangle has the smallest perimeter? _____

Day 175

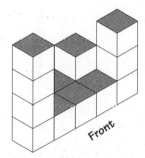

Front

Which example below **best** represents the front of this 3-dimensional shape?

Ⓐ 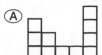 Ⓑ 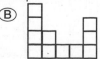 Ⓒ  Ⓓ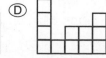

Name _____ Date _____

 Day 176 Use a stem-and-leaf plot to order the following ages of family members at a reunion:
12, 36, 48, 24, 39, 21, 47, 51, 26, 68, 75, 80, 38, 48, 9, 30, 45, 40, 27, 16, 29, 22, 35, 44, 5, 67, 53, 42, 77, 29

Work Area

 Day 177 The table shows each score at the jump rope contest.

Contestant	Score
Barbara	190
Maureen	196
Linda	254
Tyanna	166
Amesha	229

Is 207 the mean or the median score? _____

 Day 178 The table shows the number of coins in Claudia's pocket.

Coin	Number of Coins
Penny	4
Nickel	2
Dime	4
Quarter	3

Which would be a **reasonable** statement about the coins?
Ⓐ Claudia is more likely to pull out a quarter than a dime.
Ⓑ Claudia is equally likely to pull out a penny or a dime.
Ⓒ Claudia is less likely to pull out a quarter than a nickel.
Ⓓ Claudia most likely will pull out a quarter on her first try.

 Day 179 Write in mathematical form: k less than the sum of r and m.
Ⓐ $rm - k$ Ⓑ $k + r + m$ Ⓒ $r + m - k$ Ⓓ $\frac{r}{m} - k$

 Day 180 Place the following state names into two groups. Describe what each group has in common.

Alabama	Arkansas	Connecticut
Alaska	California	Delaware
Arizona	Colorado	Florida

Name _____ Date _____

Fill in the table.

	Number	0.1 more	0.1 less	0.01 more	0.01 less
1.	85.6				
2.	362.19				
3.	2.014				
4.	5.902				

5. Write 8 + 0.09 + 0.32 in standard form. _____

6. Write 0.46 + 0.3 + 0.057 in standard form. _____

7. Show 6.265 in expanded notation. _____

8. Show 40.08 in expanded notation. _____

Solve the following problems.

9. $10^0 =$ _____

$10^1 =$ _____

$10^2 =$ _____

$10^3 =$ _____

$10^4 =$ _____

10. $10^2 \times 98 =$ _____

11. $49.5 \times 10^0 =$ _____

12. $10^3 \times 1.141 =$ _____

13. $584 \div 10^4 =$ _____

14. $468.21 \div 10^5 =$ _____

15. $0.5 \div 10^1 =$ _____

Name _____ Date _____

1. The shaded part of each picture shows what fraction, decimal, and percent?

 _____   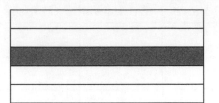 _____

2. Use base-10 units to show the following decimal: one and seven hundredths. _____

3. What best represents the shaded portion of the quadrilateral?

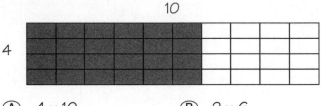

Ⓐ 4 x 10   Ⓑ 2 x 6   Ⓒ 2 x 3   Ⓓ 4 x 5

4. What percent of the flowers are in the flower pot? _____

5. Shade 0.6 of the shape.   6. Shade $\frac{6}{8}$ of the shape.   7. Shade $\frac{9}{10}$ of the shape.

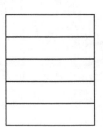   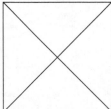   

8. Shade $\frac{2}{8}$ of the shape.   9. Shade 0.5 of the shape.   10. What fraction of the circles are **not** shaded?

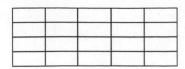      _____

Name _____ Date _____

1. Which is equivalent to $5\frac{7}{100}$?

   Ⓐ 5.007   Ⓑ 5.07   Ⓒ 5.7   Ⓓ 5.700

2. Which is equivalent to 6.70?

   Ⓐ $6\frac{7}{100}$ Ⓑ $6\frac{7}{10}$ Ⓒ $6\frac{70}{10}$ Ⓓ $6\frac{700}{100}$

3. Four-tenths of the boys in Mr. Salvatore's class wore baseball caps to school. What percent of the boys is that?

   Ⓐ 4%   Ⓑ 10%   Ⓒ 40%   Ⓓ 60%

   What percent of the boys did not wear baseball caps to school? _____

4. Laura ran 30% farther on Monday than on Wednesday. If she ran 10 miles on Wednesday, how far did she run on Monday?

   Ⓐ 3 miles   Ⓑ 13 miles   Ⓒ 15 miles   Ⓓ 30 miles

   What was her total distance for the two days? _____

5. Which is equivalent to $4\frac{9}{1000}$?

   Ⓐ 4.009   Ⓑ 4.09   Ⓒ 4.9   Ⓓ 4.90

6. Twenty-five percent of the class bring their lunches to school. What fraction of the students is that?

   Ⓐ $\frac{1}{4}$ Ⓑ $\frac{2}{5}$ Ⓒ $\frac{3}{4}$ Ⓓ $\frac{25}{10}$

7. Which is **not** equivalent to $\frac{7}{4}$?

   Ⓐ $1\frac{3}{4}$ Ⓑ $1\frac{1}{4}$ Ⓒ 1.75   Ⓓ $\frac{14}{8}$

8. Half of the houses on Blackbird Pond Road are beige. What fraction could represent the number of houses?

   Ⓐ $\frac{5}{100}$ Ⓑ $\frac{2}{3}$ Ⓒ $\frac{7}{14}$ Ⓓ $\frac{5}{11}$

9. Which of the following is **not** equivalent to $\frac{8}{3}$?

   Ⓐ 2.3   Ⓑ $2\frac{2}{3}$ Ⓒ $\frac{24}{9}$ Ⓓ $2.\overline{6}$

10. On Friday, 40% of Chip's basketball team missed practice. What fraction represents this amount?

    Ⓐ $\frac{5}{2}$ Ⓑ $\frac{4}{100}$ Ⓒ $\frac{2}{5}$ Ⓓ $\frac{1}{3}$

Name _____ Date _____

1. The perimeter of the tabletop is $15\frac{7}{8}$ feet. What is the **best** way to describe this measurement?

   Ⓐ 16 ft   Ⓒ 15 ft

   Ⓑ 10 ft   Ⓓ 20 ft

2. Last weekend the #1 movie grossed **approximately** $7 million. Which of the following is **closest** to the amount?

   Ⓐ $7.5 million   Ⓒ $6.93 million

   Ⓑ $7.08 million   Ⓓ $6.5 million

3. Antonio weighed 7 lbs 9 oz when he was born. Which weight **best** describes Antonio's weight?

   Ⓐ a little less than 7.5 lbs   Ⓒ a little less than 8 lbs

   Ⓑ a little more than 7 lbs   Ⓓ a little more than 7.5 lbs

4. Brenda works at the local grocery store. At the end of the evening her cash register drawer contained $\frac{1}{2}$ bills, $\frac{3}{10}$ coins, $\frac{1}{5}$ checks. Which list shows these amounts from **least** to **greatest**?

   Ⓐ coins, bills, checks   Ⓑ checks, coins, bills   Ⓒ bills, checks, coins

5. The finishing times for the three-legged race are . . .

   8:07   9:13   7:49   8:19

   Which list ranks these times from fastest to slowest?

   Ⓐ 7:49, 8:07, 8:19, 9:13

   Ⓑ 9:13, 8:19, 8:07, 7:49

   Ⓒ 8:19, 8:07, 7:49, 9:13

   Ⓓ 7:49, 8:19, 9:13, 8:07

Name _____ Date _____

1. Order these decimals from greatest to least.

   7.209　　　　　7.029　　　　　7.3　　　　　7.09　　　　　7.29

   _____　　　_____　　　_____　　　_____　　　_____

2. In which list are the mixed numbers ordered from smallest to largest?

   Ⓐ $7\frac{1}{2}$, $7\frac{1}{4}$, $7\frac{4}{5}$ Ⓒ $7\frac{1}{4}$, $7\frac{1}{2}$, $7\frac{4}{5}$

   Ⓑ $7\frac{4}{5}$, $7\frac{1}{2}$, $7\frac{1}{4}$ Ⓓ $7\frac{1}{4}$, $7\frac{4}{5}$, $7\frac{1}{2}$

3. Between $\frac{1}{2}$ and $\frac{3}{4}$ of the students in Ms. Mayo's class buy lunch at school. Which fraction is **within** this range?

   Ⓐ $\frac{15}{16}$ Ⓒ $\frac{7}{8}$

   Ⓑ $\frac{3}{8}$ Ⓓ $\frac{9}{16}$

   Which fraction is **not within** this range?

   Ⓐ $\frac{3}{8}$ Ⓒ $\frac{9}{16}$

   Ⓑ $\frac{6}{8}$ Ⓓ $\frac{12}{16}$

4. Which decimal rounded to the nearest hundredth is 2?

   Ⓐ 2.006   Ⓒ 1.995

   Ⓑ 2.473   Ⓓ 1.8

5. Order these fractions from least to greatest.

   $\frac{1}{3}$ $\frac{3}{6}$ $\frac{5}{6}$ $\frac{2}{3}$ $\frac{1}{12}$ $\frac{1}{6}$ $\frac{3}{12}$

   _____ _____ _____ _____ _____ _____ _____

Name _____ Date _____

1. Eric purchased leather gloves priced at $28.99. The sales tax is 6%. Which number sentence would you use to determine the tax?

   Ⓐ $28.99 ÷ 0.06 =   Ⓒ $28.99 − 0.06 =

   Ⓑ $28.99 x 0.06 =   Ⓓ $28.99 + 0.06 =

   What is the cost of the gloves including tax? _____

2. The school store ordered 5 boxes of pencils. Each box contains 144 pencils. Each pencil costs $0.29

   Write a number sentence that will show how many pencils were ordered. Then solve.

   _____

   Write a number sentence to show how much one box of pencils costs. Then solve.

   _____

3. Jaye had a discount coupon for 25% off her total sales at the supermarket. Her subtotal came to $85.73.

   What was her total with the discount? _____

   What is 6% tax on this amount? _____

4. There are 150 students signed up for ski lessons. There are $\frac{1}{10}$ the number of ski instructors as there are students.

   How many ski instructors are there? _____

   How many students will be in each group? _____

5. Zachary bought 2 sweatshirts totaling $68 before his discount. Which number sentence would you use to determine his discount?

   Ⓐ $\frac{1}{2}$ x 50   Ⓒ 68 ÷ 50

   Ⓑ 50 x 68   Ⓓ 0.5 x 68

   TAKE 50% OFF ALL SWEATSHIRTS.

Name _____ Date _____

Solve these problems.

1. 17 + 3.75 = _____   43.4 + 27.13 = _____

2. 48.7 − 5.63 = _____   62.7 − 5 = _____

3. 8.7 x 6 = _____   0.418 x 0.5 = _____

4. $ 97.02 ÷ 3 = _____   0.822 ÷ 0.6 = _____

5. It costs $2.88 to photocopy a booklet. How much would it cost to photocopy 100 times the number of booklets? _____

6. A box of 100 lollipops costs $25.00. What is the price of one lollipop? _____

7. Mr. Jones spends approximately $10.00 a day on lunch and gas for his car. At this rate, **about** how much would he spend in a year?

Ⓐ $36.50   Ⓒ $3.65

Ⓑ $3650   Ⓓ $36,500

8. Abbott School collected a total of $857.20 during a coin competition over a 7-day period. The first day, $\frac{1}{10}$ of the total amount was collected. By the third day, 50% of the total amount had been collected. By the end of the sixth day, they had collected $327.80 more than the third day.

How much was collected on the first day? _____

How much was collected by the third day? _____

How much was collected by the end of the sixth day? _____

How much was collected on the last day? _____

Name _____ Date _____

Solve these problems.

1. $\dfrac{3}{9} + \dfrac{2}{3} =$ _____

2. $\dfrac{1}{3} + \dfrac{3}{4} =$ _____

3. $\dfrac{5}{6} + 3\dfrac{1}{2}$ _____

4. $6\dfrac{3}{4} + 2\dfrac{4}{8} =$ _____

5. $\dfrac{9}{10} - \dfrac{1}{2} =$ _____

6. $\dfrac{2}{3} - \dfrac{1}{5} =$ _____

7. $14 - 4\dfrac{3}{4} =$ _____

8. $7\dfrac{1}{8} - 2\dfrac{3}{8} =$ _____

9. $\dfrac{4}{6} \times \dfrac{10}{12} =$ _____

10. $\dfrac{8}{15} \times \dfrac{9}{24} =$ _____

11. $2\dfrac{4}{5} \times \dfrac{5}{7} =$ _____

12. $\dfrac{3}{23} \times 7\dfrac{2}{3} =$ _____

13. $\dfrac{2}{5} \div 12 =$ _____

14. $\dfrac{1}{2} \div \dfrac{3}{4} =$ _____

15. $9 \div \dfrac{3}{5} =$ _____

16. $2\dfrac{2}{10} \div \dfrac{1}{5} =$ _____

Name _____ Date _____

1. The twins weighed a total of 9 lbs 15 oz when they were born. One baby weighed 4 lbs 11 oz.
    How much did the other baby weigh? _____

2. Aaron ran 3.7 miles on Monday, 4.2 miles on Wednesday, and 3.9 miles on Friday.
    How many miles did Aaron run during these 3 days?

    Ⓐ 10.8   Ⓑ 11.8   Ⓒ 10.18   Ⓓ 11.18

    How much farther did Aaron run on Wednesday than on Monday? _____

3. The table shows the number of students and the total sales in the lunchroom last week.

Day	Students	Sales
Monday	294	$755.58
Tuesday	315	$995.40
Wednesday	229	$480.90
Thursday	366	$1,039.44
Friday	421	$1,570.33
	Total	$4,841.65

    What is the daily average number of students purchasing lunch? _____

    How much more money was collected on Friday than on Thursday? _____

    What was the daily average dollar amount? _____

4. Jake bought a pair of jeans for $22.99, a shirt for $18.95, and a belt for $12.99.
    The sales tax was $3.30. He received $1.77 back in change. What dollar amount did Jake
    give the sales clerk? Show or explain how you got your answer. _____

    _____

5. You've made a New Year's resolution to exercise after school instead of watching TV. You plan
    to walk around the block as many times as you can during 1 hour. If it takes you 13 minutes to
    complete one trip around the block, how many times can you make it completely around if you
    continue at this same rate of speed? Show or explain how you got your answer.

    _____

More Practice • Solving Word Problems

Name _____ Date _____

1. Peggy and Norm collected bottles and cans to redeem at the 5-cent recycling center. They went to the recycling center 3 days in a row and received a total of $63.75 for their recyclables. What number sentence is needed to find out how many cans and bottles they turned in?

   Ⓐ $63.75 × 3 =   Ⓒ $63.75 ÷ 0.05 =

   Ⓑ $63.75 ÷ 5 =   Ⓓ $63.75 × 0.05 =

   How many cans and bottles were returned? _____

   What was the average number of items turned in daily? _____

2. Dan is buying 8 pizzas for the wrestling team. What other information is needed to determine if he is buying enough?

   Ⓐ the number of wrestlers   Ⓒ how much each wrestler will eat

   Ⓑ the number of slices per pizza   Ⓓ all of the above

3. What information is **not** needed to determine if there is a seat for everyone?

   Ⓐ There are 26 students in Mrs. Shugrue's class.

   Ⓑ There are 9 boys and 17 girls in Mrs. Shugrue's class.

   Ⓒ There are 9 tables.

   Ⓓ There are 3 chairs at every table.

4. After a day of shopping, you spent $\frac{1}{2}$ of your money. Then you bought lunch, which cost $4.50. You are left with $2.50. How much money did you start with? Show or explain how you got your answer.

   _____

5. Diane has 4 posters that are each 59 centimeters wide. She wants to put them side by side on a wall that is 3 meters wide. How much wall space will she have left over? Draw a diagram of a possible arrangement of her posters and explain how you arrived your answer.

More Practice • Writing Story Problems

Name _____ Date _____

Write a story problem for the following equations:

- *Example*

  $176.40 \div 3 = M$

  Mela and 2 friends earned a total of $176.40 for the Walk for Diabetes fund-raiser. What is the average dollar amount that each girl earned?

  $176.40 \div 3 = $58.80   Each girl earned on average $58.80.

1. $85.62 \div 0.5 = M$

_____

_____

_____

2. $\frac{1}{3} + \frac{1}{4} = M$

_____

_____

_____

3. $9.75 \div 5 = M$

_____

_____

_____

4. $8 \times 7 = M$

_____

_____

_____

5. $38.40 - 5.87 = M$

_____

_____

_____

Name _____ Date _____

1. To find the sum of 763 and 306, which expression would be a good **estimate**?

   Ⓐ 800 + 400   Ⓑ 80 + 300   Ⓒ 800 + 300   Ⓓ 700 + 300

2. To get a good **estimate** of the sum of $7\frac{3}{5}$ and $9\frac{2}{7}$, which example would be **best** to use?

   Ⓐ 8 + 9   Ⓑ 7 + 9   Ⓒ 8 + 10   Ⓓ 7 + 10

3. To find the sum of 23.71 and 8.65, which expression would you use to show this **estimate**?

   Ⓐ 23 + 8   Ⓑ 24 + 8   Ⓒ 20 + 10   Ⓓ 24 + 9

4. To subtract 106.38 from 327.75, which expression would you use to **estimate**?

   Ⓐ 400 − 100 =   Ⓑ 330 − 110 =   Ⓒ 300 − 90 =   Ⓓ 110 − 330 =

5. To find the product of $\frac{7}{8}$ and $3\frac{1}{3}$, which example would be a good **estimate**?

   Ⓐ $\frac{1}{2} \times 3$ Ⓑ $\frac{1}{2} \times 4$ Ⓒ 1 x 4   Ⓓ 1 x 3

6. To find 10% of 173. Which expression would be **best** to **estimate** this percentage?

   Ⓐ 200 x 10 =   Ⓑ 200 ÷ 100 =   Ⓒ 200 ÷ 0.10 =   Ⓓ 200 x 0.10 =

7. To find 25% of 321. Which expression would be **best** to **estimate** this percentage?

   Ⓐ 25 x 100 =   Ⓑ 300 ÷ 25 =   Ⓒ 1/4 x 300 =   Ⓓ 2.5 x 300 =

8. To **estimate** the product of 82 and 315, Julia multiplied 80 x 300. Was Julia's estimate **more** or **less** than the actual product? Why?

   _____

9. To **estimate** the difference of 2.98 and 9.52, Dante subtracted 3 from 10. Was Dante's estimate **more** or **less** than the actual difference? Why?

   _____

10. To **estimate** 48% of 47, Sara calculated 50% of 50. Was Sara's estimate **more** or **less** than the actual answer? Why?

   _____

Name _____ Date _____

1. What whole numbers would you use to **estimate** the sum of $16\frac{3}{4}$ and $9\frac{2}{5}$? Solve using the estimates.

   Estimate _____   Solution _____

2. What whole numbers would you use to subtract $7\frac{1}{8}$ from $9\frac{3}{5}$? Solve using the estimates.

   Estimate _____   Solution _____

3. What whole numbers would you use to find the product of $6\frac{1}{4}$ and $4\frac{1}{2}$? Solve using the estimates.

   Estimate _____   Solution _____

4. What whole numbers would you use to divide 37.51 by 4.3? Solve using the estimates.

   Estimate _____   Solution _____

5. Chinh wants to **estimate** the cost per ounce of a 14.5-ounce bag of tortilla chips that costs $3.29. What would be a good **estimate**? Explain your answer.

   _____

6. Matty wants to **estimate** the cost per cup of a gallon of milk that costs $2.59. What would be a good **estimate**? Explain your answer.

   _____

7. Mrs. Powell is landscaping her yard. She purchased six 40-foot pieces of edging material. She needs 90 yards of material to complete the project. **Estimate** to see if she bought enough edging material. Explain your answer.

   _____

8. Mr. Price purchased 20 square pieces of slate for his front walkway. The distance from the driveway to his front door is 40 feet. Each piece of slate is 2.5 feet long. **Estimate** to see if he bought enough slate. Explain your answer.

   _____

9. Mrs. Byrnes purchased 45 feet of rope for her clothesline. The distance between each reel is 10 yards. Is the rope long enough to go around the two reels to make her clothesline? **Estimate** to see if she bought enough rope. Explain your answer.

   _____

10. Mrs. Martin has a pool with a circumference of about 50 feet. She purchased a pool cover that is 18 feet in diameter. **Estimate** to see if she bought a large enough pool cover. Explain.

   _____

More Practice • Ratios and Proportions

Name _____ Date _____

1. The ratio of girls to boys in Mr. Muñoz's class is 5 to 2. Which of these could **not** be an example of the number of students in his classroom?

   Ⓐ 15 girls, 9 boys

   Ⓑ 10 girls, 4 boys

   Ⓒ 25 girls, 10 boys

   Ⓓ 30 girls, 12 boys

2. If the ratio of dogs to cats is 6 to 18, which would **not** be an equal proportion?

   Ⓐ 1 dogs to 3 cats

   Ⓑ 3 dogs to 9 cats

   Ⓒ 2 dogs to 4 cats

   Ⓓ 2 dogs to 6 cats

3. The table shows the number of students and the total sales in the lunchroom last week.

Day	Students	Sales
Monday	294	$755.58
Tuesday	315	$995.40
Wednesday	229	$480.90
Thursday	366	$1,039.44
Friday	421	$1,570.33
		Total $4,841.65

   What is the approximate ratio of Wednesday's sales to the total sales?

   Ⓐ 5:10   Ⓑ 1:10   Ⓒ 1:2   Ⓓ 4:4

   What is the approximate ratio of Thursday's sales to the total sales?

   Ⓐ 1:10   Ⓑ 3:10   Ⓒ 1:5   Ⓓ 1:4

4. Jed mowed 6 lawns and earned $75. At this rate, how many lawns must he mow to earn $125?

   _____

5. Margie swam 72 laps in a half an hour. At this rate, how many laps can she swim in 75 minutes?

   _____

More Practice • Computation with Percent

Name _____ Date _____

Hint: $\dfrac{\text{part}}{\text{whole}} = \dfrac{\%}{100}$

1. What is 15% of 30? _____

2. What is 30% of 55? _____

3. What is 200% of 65? _____

4. What is 80% of 40? _____

5. What is 4% of 70? _____

6. What is 140% of 300? _____

7. What percent of 365 is 73? _____

8. 18 is what percent of 75? _____

9. What percent of 145 is 58? _____

10. 42 is what percent of 350? _____

11. 220 is what percent of 400? _____

12. What percent of 40 is 30? _____

13. 62 is what percent of 310? _____

14. What percent of 65 is 45.5? _____

15. 51 is what percent of 85? _____

Name _____ Date _____

1. **Approximately** how many pounds might a 12-ton mammal weigh?

   Ⓐ 23,800 lbs   Ⓒ 1230 lbs

   Ⓑ 12,300 lbs   Ⓓ 2380 lbs

2. Erikson purchased 5 liters of soda. He filled cups with 3000 milliliters of soda.
   How many **liters** of soda does he have left?

   Ⓐ 2000 L   Ⓒ 2 L

   Ⓑ 200 L   Ⓓ 800 L

3. **Estimate** the degrees of each angle.

4. The area of rectangle A is 75 cm².   **Estimate** the area of rectangle B. _____

   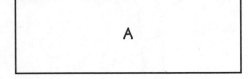

5. If the height of cylinder A is about 8 centimeters, which of the following is the **best**
   estimate of the height of cylinder B?

   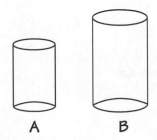

   Ⓐ 11 cm   Ⓒ 24 cm

   Ⓑ 20 cm   Ⓓ 5 cm

More Practice • Customary and Metric Measures

Name _____ Date _____

1. Complete each statement.

   4 quarts = _____ pts

   1 gallon = _____ qts

   2 cups = _____ oz

   14 cups = _____ qts

   ---

   3 tons = _____ lbs

   2000 pounds = _____ T

   5 pounds = _____ oz

   32 ounces = _____ lbs

   3.5 yards = _____ ft

   42 inches = _____ ft

   36 feet = _____ yds

   2.3 miles = _____ yds

   36.2 dm = _____ mm

   348 m = _____ km

   1.20 km = _____ m

   20 mm = _____ cm

2. The **best** unit to measure the distance from New York to North Carolina would be

   Ⓐ centimeters   Ⓑ kilometers   Ⓒ meters   Ⓓ millimeters

3. The length of a car would be **about**

   Ⓐ 4 meters   Ⓑ 4 decimeters   Ⓒ 4 millimeters   Ⓓ 4 centimeters

4. What would be a reasonable weight for a television set?

   Ⓐ 170 milligrams   Ⓑ 17 centigrams   Ⓒ 170 grams   Ⓓ 17 kilograms

5. What unit would you use to measure the weight of an elephant?

   Ⓐ ounces   Ⓑ pounds   Ⓒ tons   Ⓓ grams

6. The **best** unit to measure the length of an unsharpened pencil would be

   Ⓐ yard   Ⓑ inches   Ⓒ feet   Ⓓ miles

7. What unit would you use to measure the amount of water in a fish tank?

   Ⓐ pints   Ⓑ ounces   Ⓒ quarts   Ⓓ gallons

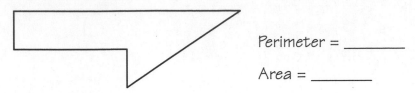

Name _____ Date _____

1. Use your centimeter ruler to determine the perimeter and area of this pentagon.

   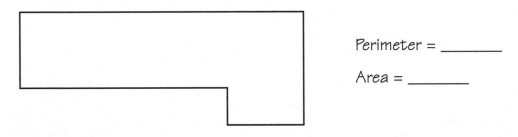

   Perimeter = _____

   Area = _____

2. What is the volume of a fish tank that has a width of $\frac{3}{4}$ of a foot, a length of 3 feet, and a height of 2 feet?

   Ⓐ 6.75 ft³   Ⓑ 6.34 ft³   Ⓒ 4.5 ft³   Ⓓ 8.5 ft³

3. The dimensions of the kindergarten classroom are 17 ft by 22 ft. How many square feet of rug will you need to purchase in order to carpet the classroom? _____

4. Use your centimeter ruler to determine the perimeter and area of this shape.

   Perimeter = _____

   Area = _____

5. The kindergarten aquarium is 7 feet long, 3 feet wide, and 2 feet tall. How many cubic feet of water would it take to fill the aquarium completely? _____

6. What is the area of a circle that has a 4-centimeter radius? _____

7. What is the area of a circle that has a 12-inch diameter? _____

8. What is the volume of a rectangular prism that has the following dimensions:

   5 cm by 7 cm by 13.5 cm   Volume = _____

9. What is the volume of a cylinder that has a 3-inch radius and a 10-inch height?

   Volume = _____

10. What is the surface area of the cylinder above? _____

Name _____ Date _____

1. Draw and label the following polygons:
   regular octagon
   regular pentagon
   rhombus
   scalene triangle
   trapezoid inside a parallelogram
   triangle inside a square that is inside a pentagon

   Work Area

2. Draw a diagonal in the trapezoid. Identify
   the two shapes you created inside the trapezoid.

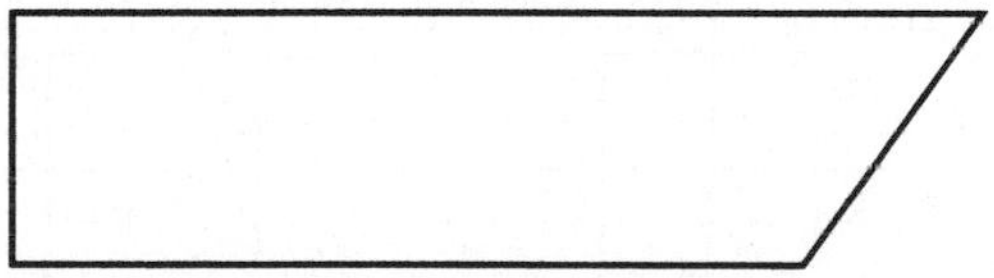

3. Draw a diagonal through each shape and describe the two shapes you created.

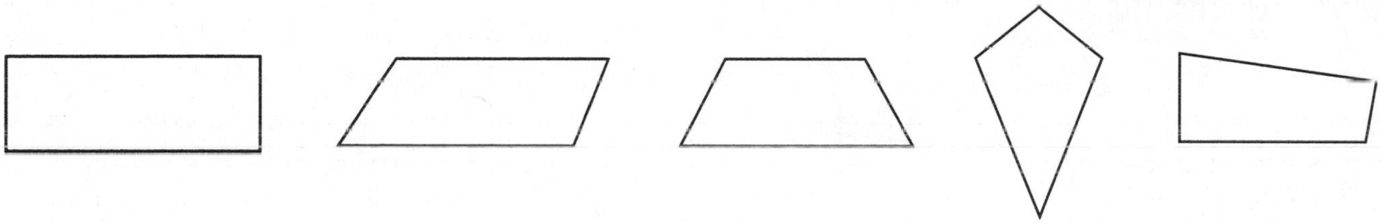

4. Which of the following describes an equilateral triangle?

   Ⓐ All angles are the same measure.

   Ⓑ All sides are the same length.

   Ⓒ There are three angles.

   Ⓓ The sum of the angles equal 180 degrees.

   Ⓔ All of the above.

5. If you put two cube-shaped dice together, what shape does it create?

   Ⓐ rectangular pyramid   Ⓒ rectangular prism

   Ⓑ triangular pyramid   Ⓓ cube

Name _____ Date _____

1. Write your first name in all capital letters. Show all lines of symmetry in each letter of your

   first name: _____ Now try your last name: _____

2. For each circle, show where the arrow would be positioned after it is rotated 90° counter-clockwise. Use the empty circle next to the figure to show the new position.

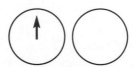 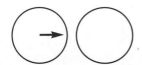 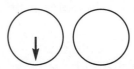 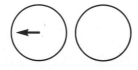

3. Which of the following shows the position of rectangle KDME after it is rotated 270° clockwise around point E? Circle your answer.

 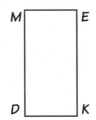 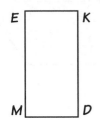 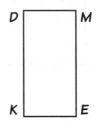

4. Draw the reflection of △ **DMB** across line x.

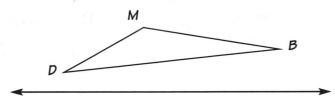

5. Sketch the congruent and similar shapes for the following figures.

   Shape   **Congruent Shape**   **Similar Shape**

More Practice • Spatial Relationships ¼ × ÷ + ¼ ×

Name _____ Date _____

1. Which example **best** represents the front of each 3-dimensional shape?

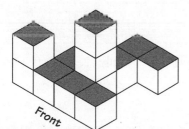

Ⓐ   Ⓑ   Ⓒ   Ⓓ

2.

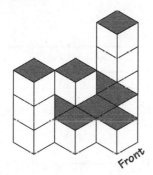

Ⓐ   Ⓑ   Ⓒ   Ⓓ

3.

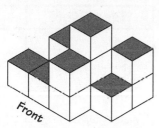

Ⓐ   Ⓑ   Ⓒ   Ⓓ

4. Plot and connect each point, in order, from the given coordinates.

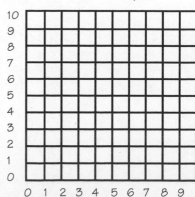

(2, 1) (8, 1) (8, 2) (6, 2) (6, 9) (4, 9)
(3, 8) (3, 7) (4, 7) (4, 2) (2, 2) (2, 1)

Name _____ Date _____

Use graph paper to display your work.

1. The table shows the increase in video rentals from 2000 to 2002. Use the information in the table to draw a **bar** graph that shows the video rentals for the 4 stores in 2002. Round to the **nearest** ten thousand.

Video Store	2000	2002
Rent One	350,276	471,832
On the Reel	274,018	468,732
Movie Blast	110,627	341,254
Video Universe	98,703	248,576

2. Sheila kept a log of how much television she watched during a 7-day period. Draw and label a **bar** graph that shows the following information.

Day	Minutes
Monday	40
Tuesday	30
Wednesday	90
Thursday	60
Friday	120
Saturday	65
Sunday	45

3. Draw and label a bar graph that shows the following information. On Monday the Snack Shack collected $\frac{1}{3}$ of Wednesday's total. Tuesday it collected $\frac{1}{2}$ of Thursday's total. On Wednesday $1500 was collected, and $1300 was collected on Thursday.

4. Use the data below to construct a **line** graph showing the number of ice cream cones sold at What's the Scoop Ice Cream Shop over a 4-year period.
   • 12,400 ice cream cones were sold in year 2. This is double the number of the first year.
   • Consumption of ice cream increased by $\frac{1}{4}$ between years 2 and 3.
   • Year 4, 250 fewer ice cream cones were sold than in year 3.

5. Use the data below to construct a **line** graph showing the number of people who attended the Middlebrook Country Fair over four years.
   • Attendance increased by $\frac{1}{2}$ from 1999 to 2001.
   • In 2002, attendance decreased by $\frac{1}{10}$.
   • In 1999, 220,000 people attended the fair.
   • In 2000, attendance increased by 17,000 over 1999 attendance.

Name _____ Date _____

1. The following results are from a survey taken of eighth graders, indicating the time they go to bed on a school night.

Time	Number of Students
9:00 P.M.	20
9:30 P.M.	35
9:45 P.M.	10
10:00 P.M.	25
10:30 P.M.	10

What time is the most popular time to go to bed? _____

Which two times, when combined, tie for third place? _____

2. The table shows the number of students, in each class, who wore red on Valentine's Day.

Class	Students	Percent
Mrs. Brennan	$\frac{15}{30}$	50%
Ms. Manoini	$\frac{16}{32}$	50%
Mr. Larkin	$\frac{13}{28}$	46%
Mr. Laudati	$\frac{14}{26}$	53%

Which class had the greatest number of students who wore red on Valentine's Day? _____

3. Tom scored an 88, 93, 89, 84, 73, 89 on his spelling tests. Find the mean, median, and mode of his test scores.   mean _____   median _____   mode _____

4. The following table shows Paradis's assists, steals, and points for the past 5 basketball games.

Game	Assists	Steals	Points
1	7	3	14
2	4	5	32
3	3	2	18
4	6	6	21
5	5	2	23

What is the **mean** number of assists per game? _____
What is the **mean** number of steals per game? _____
What is the **mean** number of points per game? _____

5. The **median** number of assists per game was . . .

Ⓐ 4   Ⓑ 6   Ⓒ 7   Ⓓ 5

The **median** number of points per game was . . .

Ⓐ 21   Ⓑ 18   Ⓒ 23   Ⓓ 14

Name _____ Date _____

Use a stem-and-leaf plot to order each of the following.

1. Number of minutes students spend doing homework each night:

   15, 30, 40, 25, 15, 20, 35, 45, 45, 50, 50, 30,
   35, 40, 40, 20, 10, 25, 35, 20, 25, 20, 35, 45

2. Number of hours on average that students watched TV
   during a 7-day week:

   5, 15, 25, 22, 15, 20, 30, 15, 5, 7, 28, 10,
   21, 18, 12, 9, 10, 10, 30, 20, 2, 20, 15, 25

3. Number of cans of soda that each student drank last week:

   8, 5, 9, 2, 5, 8, 8, 6, 4, 6, 12, 11, 20,
   9, 13, 14, 10, 12, 13, 21, 26, 23, 21, 1

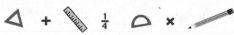

Name _____ Date _____

1. Mary has 2 pennies, 1 nickel, 3 dimes, and 2 quarters in her pocket. What is the probability that she will pull out a penny from her pocket on the first try?

   Ⓐ $\frac{2}{6}$　　　　Ⓑ $\frac{2}{3}$　　　　Ⓒ $\frac{2}{10}$　　　　Ⓓ $\frac{1}{4}$

   What percent of the coins are quarters? _____

   How much money is in Mary's pocket? _____

2. There are 3 yellow marbles, 1 red marble, and 1 blue marble in a bag. What are the chances that you'll pull out a blue marble on your first try? Show your ratio in the form of *a:b*.

   ratio _____　　　　fraction _____　　　　percent _____

3. Use this set of numbers to answer the following questions:
   　　(0, 1, 2, 3, 4, 5, 6, 7, 8, 9)
   If one number was chosen at random, what is the probability that it would be a . . .

   multiple of 2 _____　　　multiple of 3 _____　　　multiple of 4 _____

4. The spinner was spun. It landed on green. If it is spun again, what is the probability that the arrow will land on green?

   Ⓐ $\frac{1}{4}$　　　　Ⓑ $\frac{1}{2}$　　　　Ⓒ $\frac{2}{6}$　　　　Ⓓ $\frac{3}{4}$

   What is the probability that the arrow will land on yellow?

   Ⓐ $\frac{1}{4}$　　　　Ⓑ $\frac{1}{2}$　　　　Ⓒ $\frac{2}{6}$　　　　Ⓓ $\frac{3}{4}$

   What is the probability that the arrow will land on blue?

   Ⓐ $\frac{1}{4}$　　　　Ⓑ $\frac{1}{2}$　　　　Ⓒ $\frac{2}{6}$　　　　Ⓓ $\frac{3}{4}$

   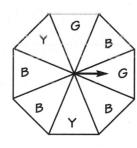

5. Which is a **reasonable** statement about the numbers on a clock?
   　　(12, 1, 2, 3, 4, 5, 6, 7, 8, 9, 10, 11)

   Ⓐ　The hour hand is more likely to point to an odd number than to an even number.

   Ⓑ　The hour hand is more likely to point to a composite number than to a prime number.

   Ⓒ　The hour hand is more likely to point to a multiple of 3 than to a multiple of 2.

   Ⓓ　The hour hand is less likely to point to a multiple of 3 than to a multiple of 2.

Name _____ Date _____

1. What are the next two numbers in this pattern?

   53, 46, 39, 32, _____ , _____

   Describe the pattern. _____

2. Find the **seventh** term in the sequence 4, 8, 16, 32 . . .

   Ⓐ 64   Ⓑ 40   Ⓒ 256   Ⓓ 128

3. Draw the figure that will be the **twelfth** in the pattern. Explain how you decided what to draw.

   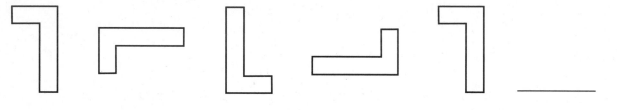

   Explanation _____

4. Examine the pattern:

   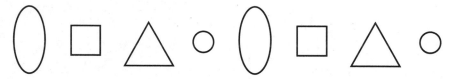

   If this pattern continues, what shape will be in the **seventeenth** position? _____

5. What are the next four terms in the following sequences?

   1, 2, 3, 5, 8, 13, _____, _____, _____, _____

   ZY, WV, SR, PO, _____, _____, _____, _____

   $\frac{1}{2}$, $\frac{3}{4}$, $1\frac{1}{4}$, 2, 3, _____, _____, _____, _____

   3, 5, 4, 6, 5, _____, _____, _____, _____

Name _____ Date _____

Solve these problems.

1. $5^2 - (16 \div 4)6 =$ _____

2. $10^3 - (6 \cdot 4) =$ _____

3. $34 - 6 \cdot 8 \div 2 =$ _____

4. $\frac{1}{5}(2 + 13) =$ _____

5. $(16 \cdot 2)\frac{3}{4} =$ _____

6. If $m \div 9 = 27$, then $m =$
   Ⓐ 3   Ⓒ $\frac{2}{3}$
   Ⓑ $\frac{1}{3}$ Ⓓ 243

7. If $m + 6.5 = 32.48$, then $m =$
   Ⓐ 25.98   Ⓒ 33.13
   Ⓑ 38.98   Ⓓ 28.83

8. If $3.2\, m = 9.6$, then $m =$
   Ⓐ 6.4   Ⓒ 12.8
   Ⓑ 3   Ⓓ 30

9. If $m - 3.18 = 5.27$, then $m =$ _____

10. If $m + 2.91 = 8.62$, then $m =$ _____

Name _____ Date _____

1. The formula for the area of a parallelogram is $A = bh$. If the base is 6 centimeters and the height is 5 centimeters, what is the area? _____

2. What is the volume of a shoe box that has these dimensions:

   $l = 13''$ $w = 5.5''$ $h = 5''$ Volume = _____

3. If the radius of a circle is 7 cm, what is the circumference?

   $C = 2\pi r$ $\pi = 3.14$ $C =$ _____

4. If the diameter of a circle is 12 cm, what is the circumference?

   $C = 2\pi r$ $C = \pi d$ $\pi = 3.14$ $C =$ _____

5. Find the area of a rectangle where $l = 2.47$ cm and $w = 13.2$ cm.

   Ⓐ 326.04 cm²   Ⓑ 32.604 cm²   Ⓒ 3.2604 cm²   Ⓓ 3260.4 cm²

6. A plumber charges $45 for the first hour and B for each additional hour. Which expression shows the correct charge for a 7-hour job?

   Ⓐ $45B + 7 =$ Ⓑ $45 + 7B =$ Ⓒ $45 + 6B =$ Ⓓ $45B + 6$

7. Donnie is 3 years older than Gary. Which expression represents Donnie's age?

   Let: D = Donnie's age G = Gary's age

   Ⓐ $(D - G) + 3$ Ⓑ $G + 3$ Ⓒ $3G$ Ⓓ $D + 3$

8. Michael was on the phone for 20 minutes yesterday and T minutes today. Which expression represents the number of minutes he was on the phone during these two days?

   Ⓐ $20 + T2$ Ⓑ $2(20 + T)$ Ⓒ $20 + T$ Ⓓ $20T + 2$

9. Robin walked 3 miles and Joanne walked 4 miles. If Tina walked W times more than the other girls combined, which expression will represent the distance Tina walked?

   Ⓐ $W(3 + 4)$ Ⓑ $3W \times 4W$ Ⓒ $3(4W)$ Ⓓ $4W + 3$

10. A mechanic charges $60 for labor for the first hour and M for each additional hour. Which expression shows the correct charge for a $4\frac{1}{2}$-hour job?

   Ⓐ $60(3.5M)$ Ⓑ $60 + 4.5M$ Ⓒ $60M + 4.5$ Ⓓ $60 + 3.5M$

More Practice • Classification and Logical Reasoning

Name _____ Date _____

1. Kharisma lives in the second house on Tremont Street. The green house is between the white house and the tan house. The blue house is not next to the white or yellow house. The yellow house is the last on the street. What color house does Kharisma live in? _____

2. Jack, Travis, Allen, and Ray brought their baseball card collection to school. Jack has 4 times as many cards as Travis. Allen has 6 times as many cards as Ray. Ray has 3 times as many cards as Travis. Which of these must be true?

   Ⓐ Allen has fewer cards than Travis.   Ⓒ Jack has more cards than Allen.

   Ⓑ Travis has more cards than Ray.   Ⓓ Ray has fewer cards than Jack.

3. Sal, Angelo, Joe, and Val are brothers. Joe is younger than Angelo but not younger than Val. Sal was born after Val. Can you arrange the brothers, in order, according to age?

   _____   _____   _____   _____
   OLDEST   YOUNGEST

4. There are lions, tigers, wolves, and monkeys in the West wing of the zoo.
   • The number of wolves is 3 times the number of lions.
   • The number of tigers is equal the total number of lions and wolves.
   • There are 6 monkeys.
   • The number of tigers is twice the number of monkeys.

   How many of each type of animal are there?

   lions = _____   tigers = _____   wolves = _____   monkeys = _____

   How many animals are in the West wing of the zoo? _____

5. Place the following shapes into two groups. Describe what each group has in common.

square	rectangle	triangle	circle
rhombus	pentagon	octagon	hexagon
trapezoid	oval	decagon	parallelogram

Day 1   1. 8.45
     2. 700 + 10 + 3 + 0.6 + 0.05

Day 2   1. B 2. D

Day 3   1. A 2. C

Day 4   C

Day 5   C

Day 6   1. 8,641 2. 11,612 3. 6,624 4. 65

Day 7   1. $\frac{2}{2}$ = 1 2. $\frac{7}{8}$ 3. $\frac{2}{6} = \frac{1}{3}$ 4. $\frac{2}{9}$

Day 8   1. D 2. C

Day 9   Possible answers:
     80 + 250 = 330 rounded to the tens place
     80 + 300 = 380 rounded to the largest place

Day 10   B

Day 11   A

Day 12   1. 300 2. 30 3. 3 4. 33

Day 13   1. B 2. acute angle

Day 14   1. B 2. C

Day 15   2 x 11 = 22 small squares; P = 26 units

Day 16   C

Day 17   ∃∣E

Day 18   Increments on vertical axis may vary.

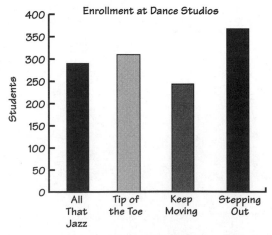

Day 19   Movie Blast

Day 20   about 50 times; Trials will vary.

Day 21   1. 25, 35, 47
     2. ⊔ T

Day 22   1. 24 2. n = 114

Day 23   5:26

Day 24   23.58, 23.38, 23.49, 23.47;
     3.167, 2.967, 3.077, 3.057

Day 25   1. 0.04 = 4 out of 100 should be shaded
     2. 0.7 = 70 out of 100 should be shaded

Day 26   1. C 2. $\frac{1}{4}$; $\frac{3}{10}$

Day 27   D

Day 28   1. D 2. 8 students

Day 29   1. $116.03 2. $37.61 3. $74.88 4. 2.401

Day 30   1. $\frac{17}{16} = 1\frac{1}{6}$ 2. 6 3. $\frac{1}{4}$ 4. $\frac{13}{10} = 1\frac{3}{10}$

Day 31   C

Day 32   1. 60 x 900 = 54,000
     2. C

Day 33   Possible answer:
     50% of 300 = 150 rounded to the
     largest place

Day 34   A

Day 35   1. 251 2. 25.1 3. 2.51 4. 303.71

Day 36   D

Day 37   1. 2 half-gals 2. 4 qts 3. 2 pts 4. 2 cps

Day 38   2 cm by 6 cm, A = 12 cm²

Day 39   1. D 2. 360°

Day 40   1. B 2. Answers will vary.

Day 41   Increments on vertical axis may vary.

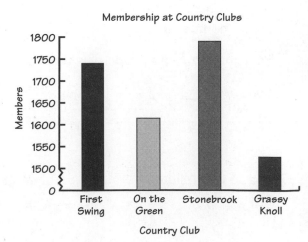

Day 42   1. Hines & Cleary 2. Gibson

Day 43   4:10 or 2:5; $\frac{4}{10}$ or $\frac{2}{5}$; 40%

Answer Key

Day 44 24, 16, 8

Day 45 **1.** 67 **2.** 12

Day 46 C

Day 47 **1.** 856 **2.** 63,000

Day 48 **1.** C **2.** D

Day 49 C

Day 50 **1.** $\frac{7}{8}$ – D

   2.
   0%   50%   100%

Day 51 **1.** D **2.** 5 boxes

Day 52 **1.** 24.625 **2.** 112.03 **3.** 1.2285 **4.** $6.09

Day 53 **1.** $11\frac{3}{4}$ **2.** $5\frac{2}{3}$ **3.** $5\frac{2}{5}$ **4.** $3\frac{2}{3}$

Day 54 15 slices

Day 55 B

Day 56 8 + 17 = 25

   8.05 rounded down

   16.6 rounded up

Day 57 **1.** B **2.** 12 pairs of white socks

Day 58 **1.** 4.8 **2.** 24 **3.** 9.6 **4.** 11.04

Day 59 **1.** right angle = 90° **2.** straight angle = 180°

   3. triangle = 180° **4.** acute angle = 1° – 89°

   5. obtuse angle = 91° – 179° **6.** circle = 360°

   7. square = 360° **8.** rectangle = 360°

Day 60 **1.** 2000 m **2.** 0.9 m **3.** 180,000 mm

   4. 7.2 dkm **5.** 0.26 cm

Day 61 Answers will vary.

Day 62 **1.** D

   2. 6 sides

   3. 8 sides

Day 63 Possible answers:

Day 64 Increments on vertical axis may vary.

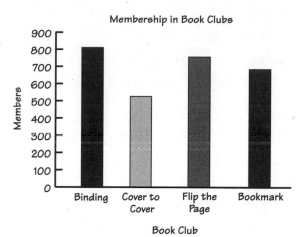

Day 65 English; 5 students

Day 66 1:4; $\frac{1}{4}$; 25%

Day 67 **1.** 49, 64; The tenth number is 121; the

   square root of the number starting with 2.

   2.

   The circles are divided into equal units

   that increase by 1 in each circle.

Day 68 **1.** A **2.** A

Day 69 5:10; $\frac{5}{10}$ or $\frac{1}{2}$; 50%

Day 70 85.24, 85.04, 85.15, 85.13;

   42.19, 41.99, 42.1, 42.08

Day 71 **1.** 1.24 = one large square and 24 out of

      100 of the second square

   2. 0.17 = 17 out of 100 of one large square

   3. 124%; 17%

Day 72 **1.** C **2.** 18 students

Day 73 A

Day 74 $1250 x 0.30 = $375

Day 75 **1.** 898.37 **2.** 1.676 **3.** 333.74 **4.** 7,510

Day 76   1. $15\frac{10}{12} = 15\frac{5}{6}$ 2. $8\frac{4}{10} = 8\frac{2}{5}$ 3. $17\frac{4}{5}$ 4. $\frac{1}{10}$

Day 77   3.7 cm

Day 78   1. B   2. $9 \times 9 = 81$

Day 79   Possible answer:
30% of 950 = 285

Day 80   49 dogs

Day 81   1. 12.5% are circles   2. 12.5% are hexagons
3. 25% are squares   4. 50% are triangles

Day 82   2400 cm³

Day 83   14 qts; 28 pts

Day 84   1. approximately 2.5 × 7.5 × 8; P = 18 cm
A = 9.375 cm²
2. 180°
3. scalene = 0 sides the same length;
isosceles = 2 sides the same length;
equilateral = 3 sides the same length

Day 85   Answers will vary.

Day 86   A

Day 87   Graphs will vary.

Day 88   62 mph

Day 89   D

Day 90   The pattern is circle, rectangle, triangle; the shading is left, right, left, right.

Day 91   1. 20   2. 35   3. $n = 11.6$ 4. $n = 184$

Day 92   1. A's = 3; B's = 12; C's = 9; D's = 6
2. 30 students

Day 93   1. 2.82   2. 5 + 0.6 + 0.03

Day 94   1. $\frac{6}{16} = \frac{3}{8}$; 0.375
2. $\frac{3}{5}$ = Shade 6 out of 10 pieces.

Day 95   1. D   2. A

Day 96 $\frac{2}{5}$; $\frac{2}{3}$; $\frac{4}{5}$

Day 97   1. B
2. total = $29.99 + $1.80 (tax) = $31.79

Day 98   1. 74,000   2. 63,000   3. 58   4. 74
5. 6.3   6. 0.0058

Day 99   1. 54   2. $4\frac{2}{3}$

Day 100   1. Monica will have enough money.
2. Steve will make approximately $1,080 in a year.

Day 101   1. More, because she rounded both numbers up.
2. Less, because he rounded both numbers down.

Day 102   Estimate 200 + 200 + 100 + 100 = 600.
But since you rounded down, Mr. Pickett needs more than 600 feet.

Day 103   1. D   2. A

Day 104   1. 29.4   2. 4.32

Day 105   ∠a = 45°; ∠b = 135°

Day 106   1. B   2. pound

Day 107   1. A = 300 ft²   2. P = 80 ft

Day 108   having exactly the same shape and size

Day 109   having the same shape and proportional corresponding dimensions

Day 110   Graphs will vary.

Day 111   1. mean = 36 minutes
2. median = 37 minutes

Day 112   A

Day 113   72, 90, 108, 126

Day 114   1. A   2. C

Day 115   Possible answers:
AE vowels, BCDFGH consonants;
AEFH = only straight line segments,
BCDG = curved lines

Day 116   1. 8.72   2. 100 + 6 + 0.007

Day 117   1. Shade 2 out of 5.   2. $66\frac{2}{3}\% \approx 67\%$

Day 118   1. B   2. D; $20.80

Day 119   1. B
2. 27.17, 27.154, 27.0976, 27.08, 27.063

Day 120   1. 0.20 × $350 = $70   2. $22 × 12 = $264

Day 121   1. B   2. A

Day 122   1. $8\frac{5}{16}$ 2. $1\frac{1}{12}$

Day 123   Answers will vary.

Day 124   1. 20 ÷ 5 = 4; Each number was rounded up.
2. More, because he rounded both numbers up.

Day 125   1.5 yds by 3 yds = $4\frac{1}{2}$ ft by 9 ft
Her fabric is too short.

Day 126   **1.** 10:15 or 2:3   **2.** 3:4 = 75%

Day 127   **1.** 10.5   **2.** 6.75   **3.** 24%

Day 128 $V \approx 270$ cm³

Day 129   B

Day 130   112 ft²

Day 131   Possible answer:

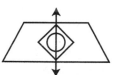

Day 132   B

Day 133

2	4, 6, 9
3	1, 2, 3, 7, 9
4	1, 7
5	1, 3, 7

Day 134   mean = $311.50

Day 135   C

Day 136   52, 84, 136; 356

Day 137   **1.** A   **2.** B

Day 138   Possible answers:
2, 4, 6, 8, 10 = even; 1, 3, 5, 7, 9 = odd; **or**
1, 2, 3, 5, 7 = prime; 4, 6, 8, 9, 10 = composite

Day 139   **1.** 519,600   **2.** 495   **3.** 3.652   **4.** 0.0584

Day 140   **1.** Shade 1 out of 5.
2. Shade 18 out of 24.
3. 2 out of 5 = 40%

Day 141   **1.** B   **2.** B

Day 142   11.52, 12.37, 11.5; 11.08, 11.5, 11.52, 12.37

Day 143 $\frac{\overset{5}{\cancel{25}}}{\underset{1}{\cancel{4}}} \times \frac{\overset{24}{\cancel{24}}}{\underset{1}{\cancel{5}}} = 30$
6.25 × 4.8 = 30

Day 144   **1.** 379,000   **2.** 190   **3.** 3.79   **4.** 1.9

Day 145   **1.** $8\frac{5}{9}$ **2.** 35

Day 146   Answers will vary.

Day 147   Explanations will vary.
1. $1.80 ÷ 3 = $0.60 per liter
2. $12.50 ÷ 2 = $6.25 per pound

Day 148   Round one side up and one side down, and
multiply. Both answers are higher than 64.
So, Mr. Mason did not purchase enough brick.

Day 149   **1.** $n = 45$ **2.** $n = 35$ **3.** $n = 4$ **4.** $n = 144$

Day 150   **1.** 32   **2.** 28%   **3.** 15%

Day 151   Rounding to 4" × 4" × 23":
$V \approx 368$ inches³; $SA \approx 400$ inches²

Day 152   D

Day 153 $V = 27$ cm³; $V = 1749$ cm³

Day 154   Possible answers:

Day 155   D

Day 156

6	3
7	6, 8, 9
8	2, 5, 7, 8, 8, 9
9	5, 5, 8

Day 157   **1.** mean = 5.2   **2.** median = 4

Day 158   D

Day 159   T, J, Q, M

Day 160   D

Day 161   Possible answers: ostrich, giraffe = animals
with long necks; **or** tiger, elephant, eagle,
bear, horse, monkey, alligator = animals
with short necks

Day 162   **1.** 608.9   **2.** 32,774   **3.** 0.009841
4. 8.21462

Day 163   Possible answers:
1.   **2.**
   40%   25%
3. $\frac{4}{12} = \frac{1}{3}$ not shaded

Day 164   **1.** $4\frac{2}{3}$; $4\frac{3}{4}$; $4\frac{5}{6}$ **2.** $14\frac{1}{4}$ mi

Day 165   **1.** $70 × 0.10 = $7 discount
2. $63 × 0.06 = $3.78 tax;
   $63.00 + $3.78 = $66.78

Day 166   **1.** C   **2.** A

Day 167 $\frac{1}{6}$

Day 168   **1.** 11:45 A.M.; 4:35 P.M.
2. This plan isn't fair. The person doing chores
on the odd day will do chores two days in a
row for the seven months that have 31 days.

Answer Key

Day 169 $3.00 ÷ 13 = $0.23 per oz

Day 170 B

Day 171 1. 28 cm 2. 14 times larger

Day 172 1. 90 3-L bottles
2. 135 2-L bottles
3. 270 1-L bottles

Day 173 1. $V = 3077.2 cm^3$ 2. $V = 49.455 m^3$

Day 174 1 by 36, P = 74 (largest);
2 by 18, P = 40;
3 by 12, P = 30;
4 by 9, P = 26;
6 by 6, P = 24 (smallest)

Day 175 C

Day 176

0	5, 9
1	2, 6
2	1, 2, 4, 6, 7, 9, 9
3	0, 5, 6, 8, 9
4	0, 2, 4, 5, 7, 8, 8
5	1, 3
6	7, 8
7	5, 7
8	0

Day 177 mean

Day 178 B

Day 179 C

Day 180 Possible answers:
Alabama, Arizona, California, Colorado, Connecticut = 4 syllables in name; Alaska, Arkansas, Delaware, Florida = 3 syllables in name; **or** Alabama, Arkansas, Connecticut, Delaware, Florida = east of Mississippi River; Alaska, Arizona, California, Colorado = West of Mississippi River.

PRACTICE PAGES

Page 43
1. 85.7, 85.5, 85.61, 85.59
2. 362.29, 362.09, 362.2, 362.18
3. 2.114, 1.914, 2.024, 2.004
4. 6.002, 5.802, 5.912, 5.892
5. 8.41
6. 0.817
7. 6 + 0.2 + 0.06 + 0.005
8. 40 + 0.08
9. 1; 10; 100; 1000; 10,000
10. 9,800
11. 49.5
12. 1,141
13. 0.0584
14. 0.0046821
15. 0.05

Page 44
1. $\frac{5}{10} = 0.5 = 50\%$; $\frac{1}{5} = 0.2 = 20\%$
2. 1.07 = 1 large square and 7 small squares
3. C
4. $\frac{3}{5} = 60\%$
5. Shade 3 out of 5.
6. Shade 3 out of 4.
7. Shade 90 out of 100.
8. Shade 5 out of 20.
9. Shade $1\frac{1}{2}$ pieces.
10. $\frac{3}{10} = 30\%$

Page 45
1. B
2. B
3. C; 60% did not wear caps
4. B; 23 miles
5. A
6. A
7. B
8. C
9. A
10. C

Page 46
1. A
2. C
3. D
4. B
5. A

Page 47

1. 7.3, 7.29, 7.209, 7.09, 7.029
2. C
3. D, A
4. C
5. $\frac{1}{12}$, $\frac{1}{6}$, $\frac{3}{12}$, $\frac{1}{3}$, $\frac{3}{6}$, $\frac{2}{3}$, $\frac{5}{6}$

Page 48

1. B; $28.99 + $1.74 = $30.73
2. 5 x 144 = 720 pencils;
   144 x $0.29 = $41.76
3. $64.30; $3.86
4. 15 ski instructors; 10 students in each group
5. D

Page 49

1. 20.75; 70.53
2. 13.07; 57.7
3. 52.2; 0.209
4. $32.34; 1.37
5. $288.00
6. $0.25
7. B
8. 1st day = $85.72; 3rd day = $428.60;
   6th day = $756.40; last day = $100.80

Page 50

1. $\frac{9}{9}$ = 1
2. $\frac{13}{12}$ = $1\frac{1}{12}$
3. $3\frac{8}{6}$ = $4\frac{1}{3}$
4. $8\frac{10}{8}$ = $9\frac{1}{4}$
5. $\frac{4}{10}$ = $\frac{2}{5}$
6. $\frac{7}{15}$
7. $9\frac{1}{4}$
8. $4\frac{6}{8}$ = $4\frac{3}{4}$
9. $\frac{5}{9}$
10. $\frac{1}{5}$
11. 2
12. 1
13. $\frac{1}{30}$
14. $\frac{2}{3}$
15. 15
16. 11

Page 51

1. 15 lbs, 4 oz
2. B; 0.5 mi

3. 325 students; $530.89 more on Friday;
   Average amount = $968.33
4. $22.99 + $18.95 + $12.99 + $3.30 + $1.77 = $60.00
5. 60 ÷ 13 = 4.6 laps, 13 x 4 = 52 min. 4 times
   with 8 min. to spare.

Page 52

1. C; 1275; 425
2. D
3. B
4. $14.00; work backward:
   $2.50 + $4.50 = $7.00 + $7.00 = $14.00
5. 64 cm of wall space left over

Page 53

Answers will vary.

Page 54

1. C
2. A
3. D
4. B
5. D
6. D
7. C
8. Less, because both numbers are rounded down.
9. More, because both numbers are rounded up.
10. More, because both numbers are rounded up.

Page 55

1. 17 + 9 = 26
2. 10 − 7 = 3
3. 6 x 5 = 30
4. 40 ÷ 4 = 10 using compatible numbers
5. $3.00 ÷ 15 = $0.20 an ounce, compatible numbers
6. $2.60 ÷ 16 = about $0.16 per cup
   Explanations will vary.
7. no: 6 X 40 ft = 240 ft = 80 yds
8. yes: 20 x 2 = 40 ft
9. no: 10 yds + 10 yds = 20 yds = 60 ft
10. no: 18 x 3 = 54
    The value of pi was rounded down to 3.

Page 56

1. A
2. C
3. B; C
4. 10 lawns
5. 180 laps

Page 57

1. 4.5
2. 16.5
3. 130
4. 32
5. 2.8
6. 420
7. 20%
8. 24%
9. 40%
10. 12%
11. 55%
12. 75%
13. 20%
14. 70%
15. 60%

Page 58

1. A
2. C
3. 100°; 170°; 55°; 30°
4. 20 cm²
5. A

Page 59

1. 8 pts   6000 lbs
   4 qts   1T
   16 oz   80 oz
   3.5 qts   2 lbs
   10.5 ft   3620 mm
   3.5 ft   0.348 km
   12 yds   1200 m
   4048 yds   2.8 cm
2. B
3. A
4. D
5. C
6. B
7. D

Page 60

1. $P = 14.5$ cm; $A = 6$ cm²
2. C
3. $A = 374$ ft²
4. $P = 21$ cm; $A = 17$ cm²
5. $V = 42$ ft³
6. $A = 50.24$ cm²
7. $A = 113.04$ in²
8. $V = 472.5$ cm³
9. $V = 282.6$ in³
10. $SA = 244.92$ in²

Page 61

1. polygon with eight sides of equal length; polygon with five sides of equal length; polygon with two pairs of parallel sides all equal length; three-sided polygon, all sides having different lengths

2.

   right scalene Δ   right scalene Δ
   acute scalene Δ   obtuse scalene Δ

3. 2 right Δs

    2 acute Δs **or** 2 obtuse Δs

    acute and obtuse Δs

   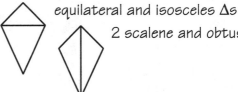 equilateral and isosceles Δs
   2 scalene and obtuse Δs

    right and acute Δs **or** acute and obtuse Δs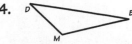

4. E
5. C

Page 62

1. Answers will vary.
2. ← ↑ → ↓
3.
4.
5. congruent = same size and shape
   similar = same shape and proportional corresponding dimensions

Answer Key

Page 63

1. A
2. D
3. B
4. 1

Page 64

1.

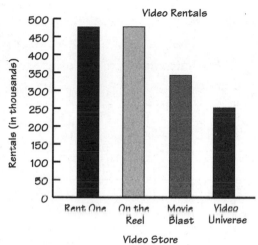

2.

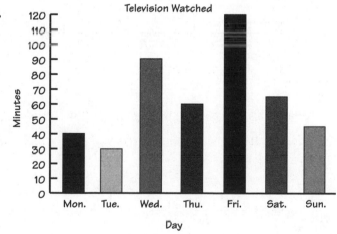

3. Mon = $500.00
Tue = $650.00
Wed = $1,500.00
Thu = $1,300.00

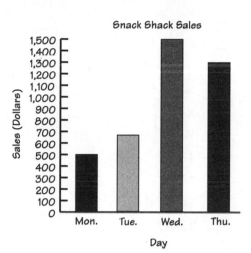

4. Yr 1 = 6,200
Yr 2 = 12,400
Yr 3 = 15,500
Yr 4 = 15,250

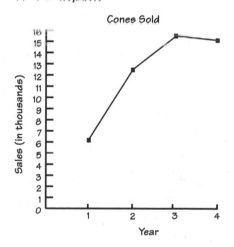

5. 1999 = 220,000

   2000 = 237,000

   2001 = 330,000

   2002 = 297,000

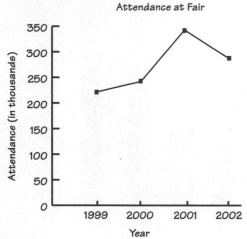

Attendance at Fair

Page 65

1. 9:30 P.M.; tie = 9:45 and 10:30 P.M.

2. Ms. Mancini's class

3. mean = 86; median = 88.5; mode = 89

4. Assists   mean = 5

   Steals   mean = 3.6

   Points   mean = 21.6

5. D; A

Page 66

1.
1	0, 5, 5
2	0, 0, 0, 0, 5, 5, 5
3	0, 0, 5, 5, 5, 5
4	0, 0, 0, 5, 5, 5
5	0, 0

2.
0	2, 5, 5, 7, 9
1	0, 0, 0, 2, 5, 5, 5, 5, 8
2	0, 0, 0, 1, 2, 5, 5, 8
3	0, 0

3.
0	1, 2, 4, 5, 5, 6, 6, 8, 8, 8, 9, 9
1	0, 1, 2, 2, 3, 3, 4
2	0, 1, 1, 3, 6

Page 67

1. D; 25%; $0.87

2. 1:5; $\frac{1}{5}$; 20%

3. multiple of 2 = 4:10 or 2:5;

   multiple of 3 = 3:10;

   multiple of 4 = 2:10 or 1:5

4. A; A; B

5. D

Page 68

1. 25, 18; each number decreases by 7

2. C

3. ⌐|

   Explanations will vary.

4. ◯

5. 21, 34, 55, 89; LK, IH, ED, BA; $4\frac{1}{4}$, $5\frac{3}{4}$, $7\frac{1}{2}$, $9\frac{1}{2}$;

   7, 6, 8, 7

Page 69

1. 1

2. 976

3. 10

4. 3

5. 24

6. D

7. A

8. B

9. 8.45

10. 5.71

Page 70

1. $A = 30$ cm^2

2. $V = 357.5$ in^3

3. $C = 43.96$ cm

4. $C = 37.68$ cm

5. B

6. C

7. B

8. C

9. A

10. D

Page 71

1. tan

2. D

3. Angelo, Joe, Val, Sal

4. lions = 3; tigers = 12; wolves = 9; monkeys = 6;

   total = 30 animals

5. Answers will vary.